WEM
BA
NYA
MA

YANN OHNONA

WEMBANYAMA

"Standing out is the only way to exist."

Contents

"Standing out is the only way to exist."

WEM BA NYA MA

PART ONE

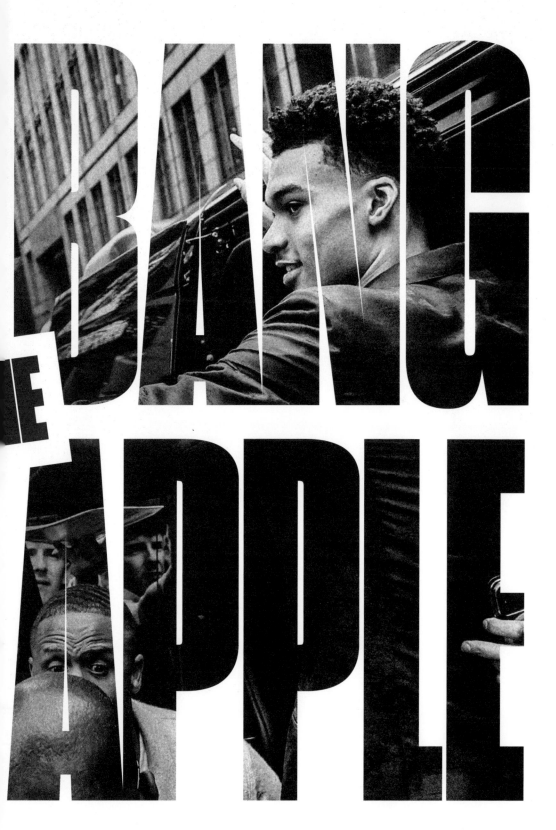

CHAPTER 1

"Establish the French reign"

ON THE NIGHT OF JUNE 22, 2023, VICTOR WEMBANYAMA BECAME THE FIRST FRENCH PLAYER TO BE SELECTED NUMBER ONE PICK IN THE NBA DRAFT. A FIRST AND LONG-PREDICTED TRIUMPH. BUT HIS ULTIMATE GOAL GOES WAY BEYOND THE AMERICAN DREAM. THE PRODIGY FROM LE CHESNAY, FRANCE, HAS ALREADY HAD A HUGE IMPACT ON ALL FRENCH SPORT AND HOPES TO EVENTUALLY TURN HIS COUNTRY INTO THE GREATEST BASKETBALL NATION IN THE WORLD.

NEW YORK—Surrounded by the incessant buzzing of yellow cabs passing up and down Times Square, a few blocks from the NBA headquarters on 5th Avenue, the face of Victor Wembanyama is plastered on billboards, his slender frame stretching over tens of yards as he buries a shot wearing the jersey of Metropolitans 92, his former French team.

June 22, 2023. After a three-day emotional whirlwind in the Big Apple, including a rockstar arrival at Newark airport, a ceremonial first pitch at Yankee Stadium and a quick dive into the local subway surrounded by the flashing phones of police officers supposedly there to protect him, it's D-Day. Or perhaps W-Day.

In just a few hours, the 19-year-old French prodigy (7ft 4in) will be summoned to the stage of the Barclays Center in Brooklyn. The outcome already a certainty

for many months, Adam Silver, head of the NBA, will read out his name before giving him a cap emblazoned with the San Antonio Spurs logo. Accompanied by fever-pitch hype not seen at the NBA since the arrival of "The Chosen One," as *Sports Illustrated* nicknamed LeBron James—with many local observers feeling the same name could apply in this instance—"Wemby" is on the verge of becoming the first French player to be selected number one pick in the Draft.

This is the starting point of a career which almost everyone believes will make history—interestingly, there have rarely been so few "haters" denouncing the arrival of such a high-profile athlete. His head already in the clouds, on board a plane above the Atlantic taking him to his destiny, on Monday, June 19, 2023, Victor Wembanyama granted

French sports daily *L'Équipe* a rare interview. In his view, "every record—even Wilt Chamberlain's 100 points in 1962—is made to be broken."

While he preferred not to get ahead of himself and reveal what he thought a successful first season or career might look like—although he did say "as many rings as possible"—he revealed one of his dreams: to make France the greatest basketball nation in the world. Or as he succinctly put it: "Establish the French reign."

How did you sleep in the final days before your departure to the US?
[*Laughs*] Well, but I've not had much of it since the end of the season [defeat in the final playing for Boulogne-Levallois Mets 92 against Monaco]. During the year, I can't sacrifice a minute of sleep for anything whatsoever if it's not related to basketball. Now, with all the organization needed for the Draft, I'm sleeping a lot less. It's not a question of stress. Although I'm sure the excitement will stop me from getting any rest the night before.

As the big day approaches, have you received any special gifts?
I've never had so many people simultaneously telling me that they were proud of me, sending me messages. I got to see close family before leaving, barring my sister [Ève] who's in the French 3x3 team.

She'll join us later. Rather than getting a physical thing, my gift was being able to spend some time with them.

We know you're a great reader. Do you have time for it?
Of course. I've finished the first two books in The Stormlight Archive. Massive tomes of 850 pages each.

I devoured them, and last week did the same with volume two of *The Witcher* [two heroic fantasy series, one of his favorite genres]. And I'm now reading *The Three-Body Problem* [a Chinese series], which is sci-fi, but not in the traditional sense. I need things to be different, to not feel like I've seen or read them before. And that goes for everything. It's one of the keys to my existence.

Your current existence is about to change. Is this the first day of your new life?
[*Ponders*] No. I think the first day will be June 22, the Draft night. That will mark the division between my old life and the new one.

Tell us about your transition into this new era. We saw you were very emotional when the Mets played in Nanterre, your first pro club, for example (May 8, 2023).
I'm not ashamed to cry, it's just another way of expressing your emotions, like laughing. I don't hold back, I feel free. There's no reason to hide it. It was amazing, with fans I've known for years still sitting in the same seats, who'd come to say goodbye.

"Wembyyy! Wembyyy!" This was the chant heard throughout the arenas of France, all packed to the rafters, as the first part of your career came to a close. What does it mean to you?
It's a crazy thing. During the match, it's hard to think about it, but when I see the images afterwards, I get goosebumps. It's special to have that kind of impact on people, even when you don't know them, and even if they couldn't get a seat—I know

The Wembanyama family at the foot of the giant screens in Times Square: from left to right, younger brother Oscar, older sister Ève, Victor, and their parents Élodie de Fautereau and Félix Wembanyama.

it was hard to find one sometimes [*Laughs*] —I hope I'll always be able to get France buzzing like that. I have no regrets. With Metropolitans 92, we did something that had never been done before. It's not the end, but a beginning.

What do you mean by that?
I'm not just talking about me. In terms of French basketball and its place on the world stage, I hope that people will soon see there's a distinction between everything that's happened before now, and everything that's starting today. I hope that all of us working together can establish the French reign.

Can you say more about that?
I want a French reign, not like Napoleon [*bursts out laughing*], but simply for France to become the greatest basketball nation in the world and for the long term. That people think of us like that. That we overtake the USA, that they're the ones saying before a competition: "We have to go and beat France." We've got the Olympic Games in Paris, and then in Los Angeles. A cycle maybe? It's impossible to say. Only time will tell.

In an ESPN article you said you want to beat the US in the final of the Paris Olympics.
That was taken out of context. I don't imagine I said it as specifically as that. Of course, as an athlete in a national team it would be a dream to beat the greatest nation in the final. But put like that, it sounds like a provocation.

13

> ## 66 I believe there are certain patterns in the universe, and that one way to achieve your dreams and self-fulfillment is to follow those patterns."

And you don't want to be provocative?
Actually, I can sometimes be like that, but I need to control it. [*Laughs*]

Let's come back to the Draft. In a press conference for the French national team, you said you've been preparing for everything that's happening to you "since you were born." What do you mean by that?
You can have this dream and these goals inside you from birth. I think I've always had that desire and yearning. Not consciously in my early years, of course. But it's something that lives inside me and it's what keeps me moving forward.

After the Draft Lottery on May 16, you also said: "the universe told me" (that it would be San Antonio).
I trust in my convictions and it's always paid off. Lots of things have happened in my life that I don't see as coincidences. I was sure the Spurs would get first pick. And I'm certain about other things too. But talking about it beforehand can ruin the script. [*Laughs*] For example, I had dinner with Michael Rubin [American high priest of sports merchandising and multibillionaire CEO of the company Fanatics, which has signed a deal with Victor]. I spoke to him about my theory and later that night I made a video of my prediction for the Lottery. I only showed it to people afterwards.

Have you planned to wear anything special for the big moment—an object or accessory?
It will be a surprise. I'll wear something that represents me, that says something about who I am. People who know me really well, or take a keen interest in who I am and what I want, could guess what it is.

How do you imagine the moment when you walk on stage?
First of all, you don't want to trip over. I think that's already happened? I prefer not to think about it. [*Laughs*] Clearly, there's a mystique, an energy around the Draft. When you think hard about something for a long time, you can almost touch it. The moment I hear Adam Silver say that sentence will be powerful because it's been building in me for years.

This will be a record Draft for France if you're pick number one, and three players are chosen in the first round.
The previous highest was Killian [Hayes, 7th in 2020], right? He may well be beaten, and … [*laughs*] not even by me [a reference to Bilal Coulibaly who in the end was picked 7th, the same position as Hayes].

You like to sing the praises of Bilal.
It's natural to big up a friend. And most importantly, it's genuine. People have really underestimated him.

How do you see the NBA game you'll soon be confronted with, particularly after dealing with ultraphysical defenses in the French Betclic Élite league, where players push the limits, for example Charles Kahudi (ASVEL, in the semifinal) and John Brown (Monaco, in the final). Will you feel finally free?
I'm not going to lie; I did sometimes find the court got too small in France. Some things are allowed there that won't be permitted in the NBA. But it doesn't bother me that I went through that. They're just two different sports. I think I'll thrive in the NBA, with more space and fewer double

teams. One world isn't better than the other. There are better players in the NBA, but the EuroLeague is superior in terms of tactics and coaching. But then there are US teams that focus more on those areas anyway, such as San Antonio. I've got nothing to worry about. I'm sure one day I'll end up in one of those teams. [*Bursts out laughing*]

Have you looked into the history of the Spurs in the 2013–2014 season when they were champions with Tony Parker and Boris Diaw?
I know about it, of course. And it's one of the greatest stretches of basketball I've had the pleasure of watching. It's the perfect example and epitome of collective play, where everyone makes their teammates better. And winning five titles in such a short time [1999, 2003, 2005, 2007, 2014],

that says something. Tony Parker sent his congratulations and wished me luck. For me, being in a franchise where there's that French tradition, the history with TP, Gregg Popovich, and above all the culture, it's an advantage because it guarantees stability. It's the best place for me.

And they also had some of the greatest players in history—Tim Duncan (number one pick in the 1997 draft) and David Robinson (first pick in 1987). Can you imagine overtaking them one day?
I'm going to have to work on my bank shot! [Duncan's signature shot, at a 45-degree angle to the board]. Tim is underrated by the people who rank the best players in history because he's not flashy enough. Of course, being the greatest is something that builds over time. I can't say that today. My first goal is to be the strongest on the court, day after day.

What's your objective in the NBA—to become a kind of European Michael Jordan?
There's no point in trying to go too fast. Before thinking about revolutionizing anything, I want to be the one who works the hardest and is most committed to building my own story and that of my team.

It seems impossible, but are you dreaming of the title in your first season?
Of course I want it. But only as a competitor. I don't know the NBA well enough yet. I haven't even played a game. I'll approach the season with humility, trying to learn as much as possible so we can win as quickly as possible.

Would the Playoffs make you happy?
We'll see.

What would a successful career look like?
I don't have the answer yet.

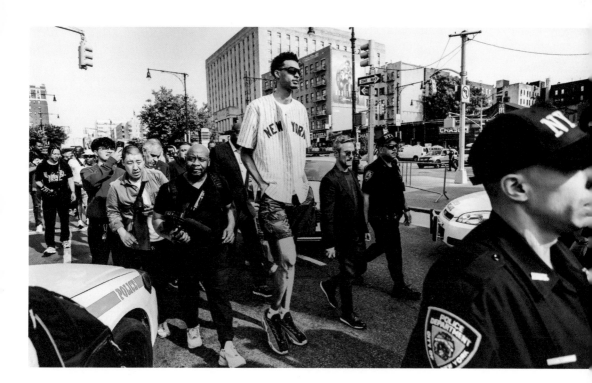

" The sole purpose of all of this is to take care of my loved ones, and if I can, to change people's lives."

You like to stand out. How will you do that in the ultracompetitive setting of the NBA?
Standing out is the only way to exist. How? By being 100 percent myself, a player who breaks the mold, and who also wins as many rings as possible.

Does that include revolutionizing playing positions and developing on the wing, or even in a playmaking role?
Vincent Collet [France national team coach] made me work hard on the point guard position and I did sometimes play there. I don't see that as a revolution. It's a personal

vision, my personality. No one can stop me from trying to develop in all positions.

Do records like Wilt Chamberlain's 100 points in 1962 fire up your competitive instincts?
Of course. Although some of them like his one are really challenging, every record is made to be broken.

Winning with multiple franchises or spending your whole career in the same colors. What does your dream career path look like?
Loyalty is an important principle in sport

and one I'm committed to. That's why I stayed with Nanterre for such a long time [from 2014 to 2021], even though I could have gone to Barcelona or somewhere else much earlier. But honestly, not even being a rookie, I don't have a say in this yet. I don't know what tomorrow will bring.

All observers of the sport seem to think the fear of injury hangs over you like a sword of Damocles. Is that a worry for you?
Not at all. Compared to other players of my size, as always, I do things differently. There haven't been other players like me so there's no benchmark. What we think we know needs to be rethought. With Guillaume

[Alquier, his physical trainer], for example, we work on ranges of movement that are close to actual injuries, so my body is prepared for extreme situations.

You're already a star. But what type of star do you want to be? American-style bling or an MVP like Nikola Jokić who once crowned goes back to horse racing and isn't bothered about losing his champion's trophy along the way?
[*Laughs*] Between the two. I'm not interested in bling. You'll never see me wearing an expensive outfit just because it's expensive or fashionable. I only dress in what I think looks good. That's why there'll be a surprise in my outfit at the Draft. Earning money

allows you to spend it without worrying about the price of things. For a long time, I've believed that money shouldn't be an issue. And it won't be. I knew that I'd be rich. But buying luxury brands, yachts, going to exotic countries—I'm not intersted in all that. The sole purpose of all of this is to take care of my loved ones, and if I can, to change people's lives.

Vincent Collet said he was counting on you to quickly become a leader, just as Tony Parker was in his time. How does that make you feel?
I was selected for the first time against Lithuania [November 11, 2022, 90-65 win, 20 points and 9 rebounds] and was surprised by the amount of responsibility I was given right from the start. I try to be humble.

There are players more senior than me, things that have to be respected. Apart from the U19 World Cup in 2021—the defeat in the final against Team USA still eats away at me—I'd never had that kind of role. But the French team is all about devotion. If you put on the jersey, it's to sacrifice everything. I'm ready to take on any role.

One of your idols, Kobe Bryant, said he had a constant craving, a yearning, to improve and be the best. What motivates you to do all this?
The simplest answer is self-fulfillment. It's almost like a script that's been written for me. And nothing can stop me from following the script, or distract me from what I want to achieve. ●

ALREADY A GUEST OF THE FRENCH PRESIDENT

It was on Friday, June 16, 2023, late in the afternoon, between two suit fittings and his final preparations for the big trip. Victor was invited to the Élysée Palace. Accompanied by his father Félix Wembanyama, his mother Élodie de Fautereau and agent Jérémy Medjana, the player from Le Chesnay spent an hour and a half in the company of the French President, the day after his Mets lost to Monaco in the Betclic Élite final at Roland-Garros. According to his staff, Emmanuel Macron had tried to attend a game featuring the basketball prodigy on several occasions, but his attempts were repeatedly thwarted by international obligations. The president was therefore keen to sit down with Victor before he headed to the United States. Their discussions apparently focused both on the player's career and on the role he might play at the Paris Olympics— sporting, symbolic, and helping to promote the country's image—alongside the likes of Kylian Mbappé and Antoine Dupont, other huge names in French sport. The interview ended with a tour of the Élysée Palace and its offices, led by Mr. Macron himself.

Emmanuel Macron
@EmmanuelMacron

Victor Wembanyama, le premier Français numéro un de la draft NBA !

Cher @Vicw_32, tu nous fais rêver. Aucun doute : tu vas marquer l'histoire de ton sport.

4:28 AM · 23 juin 2023 · 1,6 M vues

Source Twitter

2023 WORLD CUP: SHOCK WITHDRAWAL

In the buildup to the Paris Olympics—a goal declared by Victor as one of the most important of his career—the number of times the new power forward of the San Antonio Spurs has played for the senior team is stuck at four.

Four games contested in the international qualifying rounds of the 2023 World Cup. Enough to join an exclusive club of four players with 20 points or more in their debut games, and to equal Rudy Gobert's historic record of 17 rebounds in a game, stats which are the stuff of dreams.

A "personal," "difficult," but "irreversible" decision

Then, a few days after the Draft, Wemby announced his withdrawal from the World Cup, despite his declarations of intent throughout the year and again a few days before the NBA Draft. It left many feeling frustrated—coach Vincent Collet maybe first among them. It was a "personal," "difficult," but "irreversible" decision made after talking with his camp and medical staff, the player explained to *L'Équipe*, after also missing EuroBasket 2022 to protect a longstanding injury. "It would be unrealistic in terms of development and unwise in terms of health. My goal is to be here for the next 10 or 15 years, not just in 2023. I have to prepare my body to withstand this kind of scheduling, especially with preparations for the Olympics at the end of the year. I hope people will understand. It's frustrating for me, too. The French team is central to my career. I want to win as many titles as I can with them. But this is a sacrifice I have to make."

Evan Fournier, team captain in the Euro 2022 competition, said he was "disappointed, from a selfish point of view, as I would have liked to play with him," but maintained that he understood Wembanyama's decision. "One hundred percent. I would have made the same decision. It's not fatigue or about not getting hurt. That's garbage. The more you play, the better condition you're in. But he's facing a huge upheaval. He wants to start his career properly; he has massive goals. You have to meet people, immerse yourself in the culture of the franchise. All that, with all the pressure around him. When he was at Levallois, chilled and stress-free, he didn't know what was coming. Then he realized he was going to have to work his butt off. It's a new start, and hype or no hype, your opponents don't care and your own teammates don't either. He's going to have to impose himself, prove himself, show who he is, and that can only happen with time, right there in San Antonio." Thus it will be Paris 2024 for Wemby's next time in blue.

CHAPTER 2

THE FLIGHT OF HIS LIFE

L'ÉQUIPE GOT TO BOARD THE FLIGHT TAKING VICTOR WEMBANYAMA FROM PARIS TO NEW YORK, WHERE HE SET UP CAMP THREE DAYS BEFORE THE BIG NIGHT OF THE NBA DRAFT.

PARIS AND NEW YORK—He entered Terminal 4 at Orly airport "incognito," his sleep-deprived eyes hidden behind wide sunglasses, in a plain black tracksuit emblazoned with the Nike Swoosh, hood up. But there was little chance that Victor's 7ft 4in frame would go unnoticed. Especially not with several luggage carts in tow, piled high with a dozen suitcases, eight belonging to the basketball player alone. In the check-in line, we see him tenderly hugging his mother, Élodie.

Feeling emotional, Wemby? Not really, considering the journey he's about to undertake across the Atlantic on this Monday, June 19, three days before the big night of the NBA Draft, which will crown him the first French number one in history. In other words, the first day of the rest of his life. "That will be on the night of the pick. Right now, I'm not overexcited, quite calm in fact," he says, smiling, as he takes the escalator to the departure lounge.

The repeated stares, by turns astounded and admiring, followed by requests for selfies, have already started. Everywhere he goes, heads turn, gazing up toward the ceiling. "He's already impressive when you see him on TV. But wow, in person ..." says an awestruck security officer as Wembanyama tilts his head at right angles to get under the metal detector gate.

Since he played and lost in the third game of the final against Monaco on June 15 in the stunning setting of Roland-Garros (88-95), the pace of the last few days has been crazy: packing up his belongings, various organizational obligations and finalization of details in the run-up to the big day, and a meeting with French President Emmanuel Macron followed by a tour of the Élysée Palace. Accompanied by his mother, his agent Jérémy Medjana—"done in" with fatigue—and a team that's been following his every move since the start of the season

Victor Wembanyama's arrival in Newark airport, three days before the NBA Draft.

in order to make an upcoming documentary on his story, Wembanyama sits next to the emergency exit of the A321 NEO aircraft operated by airline La Compagnie which flies only business class. Seventy-six people share the star's flight, regularly looking over at the icon in the making. "It's an honor to welcome such a big celebrity, especially for someone like me who's a fan of the NBA," explains Inès Ammar, station manager for La Compagnie in Paris. "We treat everyone with high standards, but as a VIP we're giving him special attention, especially if he or his team have any special requests." On its Instagram account, the company writes the following message to the NBA: "We'll take good care of him until we get to New York!"

A bit of reading, a gourmet meal followed by a nap, then a 45-minute interview with sports daily *L'Équipe*—Wembanyama's journey is peaceful and relaxed. The player takes a souvenir photo with the crew and exits the Airbus. What happens next is anything but peaceful. On his arrival, Newark airport in New Jersey is already buzzing with excitement as "Wembamania" takes hold.

In the corridors, more and more people ask for selfies, their persistence growing. Several point their smartphones as he passes to try and capture the moment, before running away giggling. A blurred result guaranteed! At the baggage counter, Wembanyama counts his suitcases eight or ten times—it would not do to forget an outfit at the airport.

"Hurry up, or everyone will be after him," urges Medjana, who has seen what's brewing up ahead. Clusters of supporters—around a hundred—have gathered in front of the terminal exit. Scanning social media for the tiniest clue, the most determined fans had no trouble identifying the flight and arrival time of their new hero. Some are already wearing San Antonio jerseys emblazoned with Wembanyama's name and the number one. "It doesn't exist yet, the Spurs don't have the right to sell it," admit Frankie and Nathan, who say they have come straight from Florida and Tennessee to witness Wembanyama's arrival at the NBA, and who bought counterfeit jerseys from a Philippine website for $25 each. "You want one?" asks one of the rogues with a smile.

Kitted out with jerseys, but also basketballs, pictures, and other merchandise, a swarm of fans—or future resellers on the black market, the famous "scalpers," and it's impossible to say who's who—throw themselves on Wembanyama, who willingly embraces an impromptu signing session in a frenzied atmosphere of relative good humor. Meanwhile the cameras of the American media record it for posterity.

Extricating himself from the crowd takes a few minutes, causing the luggage porter who has lost sight of the delegation to break out in a cold sweat. They eventually reappear and make a dash for two black vans with tinted windows. Next stop the Westin hotel, where all players attending the Draft are staying. Several unknown vehicles follow in their wake and turn up as they arrive, with a new welcoming committee ready to greet the Frenchman. This time he heads straight for the lobby and joins his family in a private room while the security services finish evicting the onlookers and autograph hunters.

Just a block away from Times Square, where his face is already displayed on the flashing screens in the beating heart of the Big Apple, Victor Wembanyama ain't seen nothin' yet. ●

CHAPTER 3

THE WAY OF THE KING

THE VICTOR WEMBANYAMA ROCKET LIFTED OFF ON THE NIGHT OF JUNE 22, DESTINATION SAN ANTONIO AND THE STARS. THIS IS A REPORT ON FOUR SURREAL DAYS IN THE HEART OF THE BIG APPLE, BEFORE THE FIRST PICK OF THE 2023 DRAFT TOOK OFF FOR THE SOUTH.

NEW YORK AND SAN ANTONIO

ONE SMALL STEP FOR MAN

When the clock started ticking on the giant screens at the Barclays Center in Brooklyn, Wemby's life's dream had never felt so close. The stage where Adam Silver, boss of the NBA, was about to say his name, had never been so near.

Victor is squeezed into his chair, acting as master of ceremonies at the end of a table surrounded by his family: Félix Wembanyama, his father; Élodie de Fautereau, his mother; Oscar and Ève, his brother and sister; Bouna Ndiaye and Jérémy Medjana, his agents; Issa Mboh, his press manager, and Clémence, his godmother. With a golden basketball in his hands, he is becoming impatient with excitement, and the wait is unbearable. Before announcing its choice in the Draft, each team must observe a regulatory and mandatory time delay of five minutes. Three hundred dizzying seconds that feel like an eternity.

"Longest five minutes of my life," the player from Le Chesnay would later say. "This is where I started getting the butterflies. It's where I started seeing my family get silent, everyone looking at their watch." Wemby tries to contain his agitation, turning around to examine the room from where an indistinct chant has been rising and falling nonstop for two hours: "Wemby! Wemby!"

In the green room, an area demarcated for the favorites in the first round, euphoric and diminutive kids are messing around between the tables at the foot of the main stage, wearing XXL jerseys of the power forward.

A STONE'S THROW FROM MADISON SQUARE GARDEN, ON A GIGANTIC BILLBOARD ON 34TH STREET, THE FACE OF VICTOR WEMBANYAMA SLOWLY FADES IN, FOLLOWED BY THE SLOGAN: "HELLO HUMANS."

Shortly before the fateful moment, he shook Joakim Noah's hand and shared a few words with the former international center of the Chicago Bulls. He also got a video call from Nicolas Batum and other French players in the NBA keen to welcome him to his new family.

A microphone boom sits above the table of the former Nanterre and Mets player to capture the tiniest snatches of conversation between the guests. As the seconds tick by, a dozen cameras gradually approach the family and eventually surround it, making the space and the moment even more suffocating.

Then at last, liberation. Silver returns to the stage and delivers the iconic sentence: "With the first pick in the 2023 NBA Draft, the San Antonio Spurs select ... Victor Wembanyama, from Nanterre, France."

At least that's what he seems to have said, as the audience immediately erupts into applause and the commissioner's words become completely inaudible.

"He actually said 'from Nanterre,'" repeats an unbelieving and tearful Frédéric Donnadieu, Wemby's first coach in his first pro club (2014–2021), and one of the rare guests invited to the USA by the new "chosen one." "I met Adam Silver this afternoon and

he let me know I'd be getting a surprise. It was Victor who insisted he said he was from Nanterre—not from Le Chesnay, his home town. From a selfish point of view, this is absolutely massive for our club. And a gift from Victor that has touched me deeply. And then the green of his suit … When I met him later, he smiled and asked me: 'Well? You happy?' I felt like a privileged witness to a historic moment."

As expected, on the night of June 22, Wemby is named the first ever French number one pick in an NBA Draft. Hugging his guests one by one, he walks the 50 yards separating him from the steps. Then the man LeBron James nicknamed the "alien" dons his cap emblazoned with the spur and without stumbling—as if levitating—he takes his first steps on the moon.

"Being seated at this table of the first pick in the Draft is a big message of hope for millions of people," says Bouna Ndiaye. "Jérémy [Medjana] and I had nothing more than other people. We believed in ourselves, and worked, worked, worked. We managed to put Bilal [Coulibaly] and Rayan [Rupert] on adjacent tables. For years, people told us we didn't know what we were doing. But now, here we are."

At the exact same moment, a stone's throw from Madison Square Garden, on a

gigantic billboard on 34th Street, a video of a big bang explosion starts to play in a loop, launched by the Swoosh brand. The face of Victor Wembanyama slowly fades in, followed by the slogan: "Hello Humans."

A WORLD TOUR AND A "BREAKFAST TACO"

He stayed backstage for a good few moments, derailing the split-second timing of American TV. It was on the couch of broadcaster ESPN where, seeing his tearful younger brother and mother, the intensity of the moment caught up with Victor. Sobbing and comforted by his sister Ève, he shakes his head, dazed, needing a minute to compose himself. "I broke down when I saw my brother's tears. It all got very real. And yet … it's still so surreal!" says the man with a Spurs jersey emblazoned with the number one draped over his shoulders. As well as wanting to win championship titles as quickly as possible,

he says he is looking forward to experiencing the Texan tradition of the "breakfast taco" filled with scrambled eggs.

The outcome of the plot was written in black and white, the historic colors of the Spurs. But the emotional outpouring was uncontrollable and anything but monochrome. "When you're expecting a baby, you know it nine months ahead of time," jokes Wembanyama. "But then when it comes, you're still emotional. What happened to me today is iconic, legendary. Hearing that sentence from Adam Silver, I've dreamed of it so much, I could almost touch it."

After another embrace with the boss of the big league, this time out of sight of the cameras, he is handed a smartphone. The name of Gregg Popovich—the San Antonio coach—flashes up. A short discussion in French follows. Then the young Padawan—a big *Star Wars* fan in his spare time—says to his future Yoda: "I'm ready to learn. I can't wait."

"It was very casual," he commented later on the conversation with Popovich. "He's not intimidating yet. But I'm sure he's gonna get intimidating when I see him in real life." [*Laughs*]

Wembanyama reappears on the giant screens of the Barclays Center, crosses the room in the opposite direction, his eyes swollen. He embarks on an obstacle course through the labyrinthine corridors plastered with posters of past concerts held in the home of the Brooklyn Nets. Next stop is the TV studio, official podium, VIP area, cramped booths separated by black curtains that look more like voting booths, one of which is reserved for the 30 or so accredited French journalists.

Every five minutes, the "alien" lands on a different planet and answers the endless customary questions with the same relaxed confidence, as he takes an express tour of the world's media. He winks and smiles at Issa

Mboh, his press manager, whose eyes are much more tired than those of his protégé, more than two hours after the latter climbed the steps to claim his prize. "OK? All done?"

Not quite—it was just the start of another sleep-deprived night with more festivities, and the culmination of a surreal first four days in the Big Apple.

IN THE FOOTSTEPS OF JACQUES CHIRAC AND BARACK OBAMA

Tuesday, June 20, 4pm. The corridors of the New York subway at Columbus Circle station, near Central Park and opposite Trump Tower, are pulsating, and not just from the trains passing between pillars of faded paint. A 7ft 4in shadow contorts himself as he descends the stairs, inhales the acrid odor that haunts the place and regularly bends his head to pass through the corridors, escorted by a procession of a hundred people. There are the player's security staff, journalists who

"I BROKE DOWN WHEN I SAW MY BROTHER'S TEARS. IT ALL GOT VERY REAL. AND YET... IT STILL FEELS SO SURREAL!"

VICTOR WEMBANYAMA

have spread the word—mainly *L'Équipe*, the *New York Times* and French TV channel TF1—and agents from the New York Police Department (NYPD) who want autographs and selfies themselves. "Watch your bag, they don't seem very attentive," a family member whispers to us with a smile. Onlookers have also joined the crowd, including … Bilal Coulibaly, a blissful smile on his laughing face. A future number seven in the Draft, no one seems to have noticed him.

Wembanyama's hair caresses the ceiling of the crowded subway train as the merry congregation piles in to join him. "It's cool, it's a bit higher, I can't stand up in the Paris Métro," smiles Wemby, wearing a jersey emblazoned with the number five of Joe DiMaggio, legend of the New York Yankees. The crew is headed to the Bronx, where Yankee Stadium dominates 161st Street. "Welcome to New York!," "Rookie of the year!," "Victor! Look this way!" Wembanyama is accosted with every step he takes.

During the journey, the player tells his agent an anecdote. In a training session when he was 14, a ball got stuck between the hoop and the board. "I managed to touch it by jumping … but with my foot, like Kadour Ziani. I'd love to do that again some day." Then he sits down for a few minutes to do an interview for French TV.

"That trip on the subway was perhaps the coolest thing of the week. It was him who wanted to do it. He knew it was a really rare opportunity," explains Mboh. "The buzz is crazy, ten times more than what we had in France. Some people said we were hyping him 'too much.' Why do we sometimes still have this negative attitude in France? As well as what he can achieve in terms of his sport, we have a guy who can and wants to represent France. We should be proud of that."

At the subway exit, Wembanyama places his hands on either side of the ticket barrier, and with both feet joined together simply jumps over the turnstile blocking his way. Did he know that in 1980 Jacques Chirac was snapped for posterity at the Auber metro station in Paris where he too pretended to be a fare dodger?

On the dirt bordering the stadium pitch, the French player is greeted with "Go, Spurs, go!" an extremely rare sound in the Big Apple. He stops several times in front of the netting protecting the stands to high-five fans and sign photos, jerseys, and caps. He puts on a juggling show with three balls that he then throws into the stands, before disappearing into the bowels of the venue for a warmup. He has been invited to throw the ceremonial first pitch of this evening's game against Seattle. A century-old tradition that Ronald Reagan (1988), Bill Clinton (1993), and Barack Obama (2009) have all given up their time for. And the vibe around Wemby is definitively presidential.

Under the watchful eyes of Marine Johannès, the French international from the New York Liberty team, he does his best without getting the perfect pitch. Wembanyama stays to follow the game after his ceremonial duties are done, and that evening posts a photo of himself holding a baseball on his Instagram account. Clasped in his huge hands, the white sphere looks hardly bigger than a ping-pong ball. Instant global buzz.

"People were cool, friendly, a bit crazy at times on the subway," he says the next day. "But to feel the passion for athletes here, the culture, it's great. As for my pitch, the base was further away than where I'd practiced. So I threw it too wide and didn't have the accuracy." An opportunity to come back to it a bit later in his career? "I want to do everything that's never been done before. Michael Jordan didn't make it to the MLB [when he paused his career to take up baseball]. Mmm … and why not me?" he was heard to joke to one of his agents on the stadium pitch.

WEMBY DELIVERING THE CEREMONIAL FIRST PITCH IN THE GAME BETWEEN THE NEW YORK YANKEES AND SEATTLE MARINERS. A CENTURY-OLD AND PRESIDENTIAL TRADITION THAT RONALD REAGAN (1988), BILL CLINTON (1993), AND BARACK OBAMA (2009) HAVE ALL GIVEN UP THEIR TIME FOR.

" PEOPLE WERE COOL, FRIENDLY, A BIT CRAZY AT TIMES ON THE SUBWAY. BUT TO FEEL THE PASSION FOR ATHLETES HERE, THE CULTURE, IT'S GREAT."

VICTOR WEMBANYAMA

NIGHT INTRUDER AND TRADING CARDS

The week's endless list of activities includes an appearance on JJ Redick's renowned podcast, *The Old Man and the Three*, an invitation to the ABC show *Good Morning America*, a charity appearance for the refurbishment of a school in Harlem, a few shots on the legendary Rucker Park streetball court, a meeting with the players' association (NBPA), and another with NBA boss Adam Silver as part of the "NBA Experience," to which a few fans were also invited for the princely sum of … one thousand dollars. As for the Draft, certain tickets featuring backstage tours and meetings can even go for as much as $2,500 on the official website. After the event, the NBA reported that the 2023 edition had been the most watched in its history—4.9 million viewers, peaking at 6.1 million when the number one pick was announced.

His sleep deprivation is therefore off the scale. And it racks up another notch on the night before the big event, not because of stress. It's after one o'clock in the morning, in the darkness of the Westin hotel in Times Square, when the door of Victor Wembanyama's room, 4209, resonates to the sound of loud knocking from an intruder. A vacuous-looking individual with a tuft of blond hair, his belly squeezed into a Boston Celtics T-shirt, has somehow managed to locate the French player, thinking it would be wise to come and ask for a few autographs in the middle of the night. The troublemaker is quickly removed. Wemby, who got off lightly with nothing more than a scare, has to pack his things and change floors. "It's unbelievable," exclaims Medjana angrily. "This incident shows the madness unleashed by Victor since his arrival. It's beyond all understanding. It comes with a lot of positives and a few negatives. That guy managed to get in despite the deployment of a massive security operation with the hotel, the NBA, and San Antonio. What we're experiencing today is unprecedented. Like a rock star."

But there's no chance of sleeping in or time to catch his breath. The hour of reckoning approaches and he still has one box to check: Times Square. "It's hard to walk around Manhattan on my own. I'll have to run away one night and do it," jokes Wembanyama. On Thursday, June 22, a late-morning appearance is organized by Fanatics, a company specializing in trading cards and sports merchandise, which has signed a sponsorship deal with the player. To mark the occasion, it has reserved two giant screens right in the beating, flashing heart of the Big Apple. The image of Wembanyama suddenly appears on the screens just as the player extracts himself from a van with tinted windows to enjoy the view and devote himself to a family photo session inside a duly demarcated safety barrier.

THE PHILOSOPHER'S STONE AND OUTER SPACE

It's time to put on his suit. "I just closed my eyes for 15 minutes to recharge my batteries but I don't feel tired," says Wemby on the red carpet, which welcomes the class of 2023 in the style of the Cannes Film Festival. The French player has chosen an outfit in a kimono style, its deep and understated green contrasting with the sparkling bling of Scoot Henderson, his supposed rival for the top spot in the Draft. It's also the color of Nanterre, his first pro club. "Green's a color I really like," he explains. "It looks kinda outer space, you know … alienlike.

" I SAW THIS CHAIN IN A DREAM. I SPOKE TO MY AGENT ABOUT IT AND WE CONTACTED JEWELERS TO GET IT MADE. "

VICTOR WEMBANYAMA

It's a good reflection of me." Just like the surprise he announced, which takes the form of a diamond-shaped pendant enclosing a rock flashing multicolored reflections. "A bismuth," explains the young French player who takes a keen interest in lithotherapy, or the healing energy of crystals and semiprecious stones. "It's radioactive, but as long as I don't touch it, it's OK. [*Laughs*] I saw this chain in a dream. I spoke to my agent about it and we contacted jewelers to get it made."

For his custom-made clothes, Wembanyama has mainly called on the services of a French tailor, Chams, while the prestigious J.M. Weston factory in Limoges handmade his size 20.5 shoes. "A real challenge, even for them, and a meticulous piece of craftsmanship for such a large size," says Medjana. His suit was designed by Louis Vuitton and Wembanyama had the chance to meet the creative director of the men's collections, singer-songwriter and designer Pharrell Williams. Now all he had to do was to avoid falling flat on his face or slipping as he joined Silver on the platform.

After the ceremony, his family and team who had come to witness his accession—physical trainer Guillaume Alquier and Nanterre coach Frédéric Donnadieu—met in the Soho district of New York City at the Ladurée restaurant. Evan Fournier, the New York Knicks player, was also expected. Other players included Bilal Coulibaly (7th, Indiana, traded to Washington), Rayan Rupert (43rd,

Portland), and their families, with both men also in the ComSport stable. A fourth French player, Sidy Cissoko, was drafted like Wembanyama to San Antonio, in 44th spot.

"Victor was one of the first to leave. He was exhausted," says one of the lucky few. On Friday, June 23, the San Antonio franchise chartered two private flights to transport the entire delegation and that of the Spurs back to Texas. For Wembanyama, the sun had already risen on a New World. ●

wemby 13min

Lmaooooo

#3,000%
The increase in sales revenue on Spurs merchandise since the team knew it would have the chance to pick Victor Wembanyama in the Draft.

VICTOR WEMBANYAMA

CHAPTER 4

WEMBAMANIA HITS TEXAS

AFTER FOUR CRAZY DAYS IN NEW YORK, VICTOR WEMBANYAMA SET UP HOME IN SAN ANTONIO, WHERE HE WAS WELCOMED WITH WIDESPREAD EUPHORIA.

SAN ANTONIO—The sun is beating down on asphalt hot enough to melt your rubber flip-flops. But that's not enough to stop hundreds of Spurs fans from taking their positions near the airfield reserved for private planes landing in San Antonio.

The flight carrying Victor to the Texan promised land, along with that transporting his relatives and the franchise delegation present in New York for the four-day Draft extravaganza, land several hours late.

But Coyote, the team mascot, continues to bang on his drum to keep excitement levels high. Those in attendance hardly need it. Pickups decorated in the team colors display the Spurs honors list and rev their engines. There's no shortage of waving signs: "Welcome Wembanyama," "Aliens do exist," and even "My daughter's single. Marry her!" A constant chant of "Wemby!" welcomed their new superhero. Not quite yet an NBA championship parade, but certainly a nice prologue. The aircraft lands and is duly sprayed with the water cannon of local firefighting vehicles, a "water salute" reserved for historic events and distinguished guests.

"Wembamania" had already been raging in San Antonio for more than a month just like the Draft, when on May 16 the Draft Lottery designated the Spurs as winners of the first pick, meaning that after David Robinson in 1987 and Tim Duncan in 1997, they had the possibility of recruiting a potential third legendary player in Wemby. A long way from its usual standards since its last title in 2014 (with Tony Parker and Boris Diaw), the team with a strong French backstory has been living in an ecstatic atmosphere ever since the announcement. On Interstate 35, it's impossible to miss the billboard asserting: "Victor Wembanyama, you're officially a Texas boy."

Murals—painted with varying degrees of success—have sprung up on walls around the city, and mariachi bands have been busy writing songs for him. The city's storekeepers have been quick to jump on the bandwagon. Jerseys, T-shirts, beers, an unappealing "Wemby Burger" garnished with a slice of low-grade foie gras, and even candles bearing his image, are selling fast. Marcie Anguiano, founder of Mission Crafts Chandlery where she makes candles by hand in the upscale Arsenal district, had no hesitation in depicting Wembanyama in the finery of the Messiah. "This represents the light at the end of the tunnel, the light of a prodigy who can change the destiny of our team," she explained to Maxime Aubin from sports daily *L'Équipe*. The "Wemby Vela" prayer candle retails at $30 a piece.

The day after his big arrival, a first media session is held on Saturday, June 24, at the AT&T Center, packed out two days before with ecstatic fans as they followed the Draft on giant screens. Wembanyama gives a surprised smile as he leans over to discover, under the five championship banners of the Texan team and Tony Parker's retired jersey, a LEGO Eiffel Tower on the podium set up on the court, standing a good 4ft high. A welcome gift for the two French rookies, Wembanyama and Sidy Cissoko, and a nod to Wemby's love of the little building blocks.

The lights dim and presentation videos with compilations of their best moves and messages from their relatives and friends are projected on screen, as the distinguished

> ❝The last 24 hours have been emotional and tiring. I didn't expect so much attention as soon as I arrived. I already feel I belong.❞
>
> VICTOR WEMBANYAMA

guests sit on the front row of a large-scale press conference attended by some 60 journalists and 20 camera people. The Texan club has pulled out all the stops. Cissoko and Wembanyama, who have known each other since they were nine years old and competed on opposing teams in the U11 World Cup in Bourbourg in 2014 and 2015, simply look on in wonder.

"The last 24 hours have been emotional and tiring. I didn't expect so much attention as soon as I arrived. I already feel I belong," says Wembanyama, recalling the dinner held to celebrate his arrival with Gregg Popovich, Sean Elliott, Tim Duncan, David Robinson and Manu Ginobili. "One of the best evenings of my life. In a couple of hours, I learned more about the NBA than in my whole life. It's super-reassuring to know that these guys still live in San Antonio, they still gravitate toward the club, they've kept a relationship with the franchise. Tim Duncan

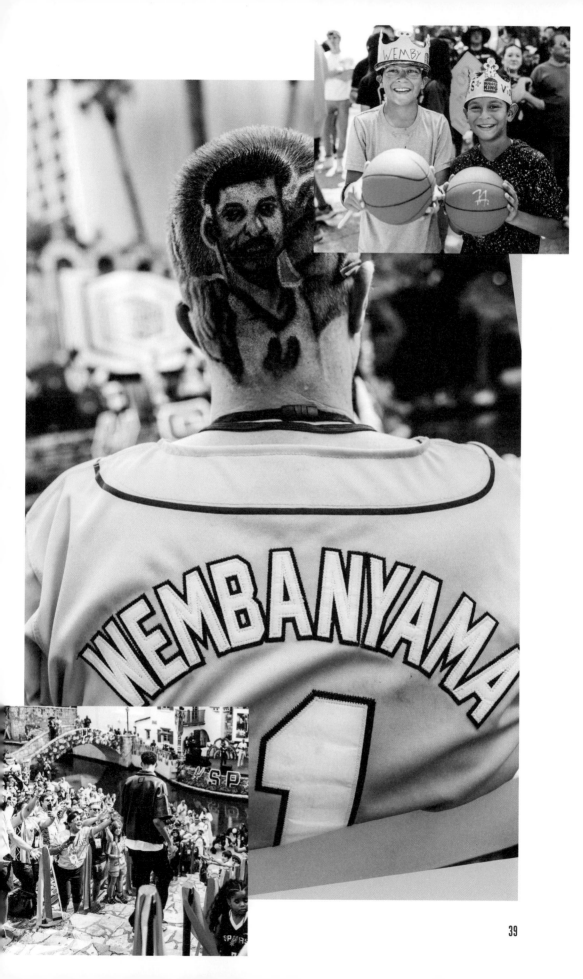

> " We've been blessed by basketball gods. We want to build a team that can sustain success for a long period of time. We're here to celebrate the future. "
>
> BRIAN WRIGHT, GENERAL MANAGER OF THE SAN ANTONIO SPURS

told me he arrived in the same conditions, with David Robinson and Sean Elliott to show him the way. It's comforting to know that there are legends, not only of the club but also of the NBA, who are there to help me and who won't let me make the same mistakes twice. Compared to a rookie ending up somewhere else, that's a huge advantage."

In an arena that has missed out on the Playoffs since 2019, hope is reborn. There are boxes overflowing with T-shirts emblazoned with the number one. Some have a Spanish flavor and are marked "El Wemby" (given the city's proximity to the Mexican border, a large percentage of the team's fanbase is Spanish speaking). Compared to the same time period last year, sales in fan stores have increased by … 3,000 percent, according to a member of the Spurs' sales staff.

To offer him the best possible support, his agents Ndiaye and Medjana have decided to move their Dallas-based American offices to San Antonio. A few hours before their official introduction, concluded with a photo and video shoot in the Spurs uniform, the two men from the Île-de-France made a first

appearance with great fanfare on the River Walk, a local tourism hotspot and pedestrian street bustling with restaurants and stores. A few lucky people, including sponsors and season ticket holders, had taken up their positions in the semicircular auditorium bordering the river. To the sound of violins, harps, and trumpets, under the gaze of "Admiral" David Robinson, the two new Spurs players made their entrance to cheers and whoops after speeches by Peter Holt, owner of the franchise, CEO R C Buford and general manager Brian Wright. "It was a long process to get to this point," says Wright. "We've been blessed by the basketball gods. We want to build a team that can sustain success for a long period of time. We're here to celebrate the future."

What next for Wembanyama? A trip to Portland and the Nike World Headquarters. Followed by the Las Vegas Summer League where he once again packed the house (two games, 9 and 27 points), and experienced some unfortunate repercussions of his popularity in a highly publicized incident with Britney Spears. Also in Nevada at the

same time, the singer tried to approach the player. But walking up behind him, and not recognized by Wembanyama's security staff, she was violently pushed back after trying to get his attention by tapping him on the shoulder.

On exiting the highly emotional media whirlwind, the player let out a big sigh of relief. "In the past month, I think basketball wasn't even 50 percent of my schedule. I can't stand it. I know it's a special moment in my life, and it was incredible to experience it, but I'm just glad it's over honestly. I just want to hoop, work out, and lift. Because this is my life." That life, in the crazy summer of 2023, was only just beginning. ●

CHAPTER 5

ADAM SILVER: A GOLDEN AGE OF BASKETBALL"

ADAM SILVER, THE NBA COMMISSIONER, BELIEVES THAT THE ARRIVAL OF VICTOR WEMBANYAMA OFFERS A UNIQUE OPPORTUNITY TO FRANCE, AS WELL AS TO THE ENTIRE BASKETBALL PLANET.

A stone's throw from Central Park, the Rockefeller Center and the NBA Store, the two neo-Gothic spires of St Patrick's Cathedral in the heart of Manhattan on Fifth Avenue look breathtaking from the vast windows lining the office of 61-year-old Adam Silver. Located on the 18th floor of Olympic Tower, the headquarters of the North American league consist of four stories of offices filled with legendary relics, such as the first championship ring awarded to the Philadelphia Warriors in 1947, and the Converse sneakers worn by Wilt Chamberlain in his 100-point game on March 2, 1962. Here, the head of the NBA, in office since 2014, talked to *L'Équipe* about the incredible breath of fresh air created by the arrival of Victor Wembanyama, not only for France but also for his league. "We're living in a golden age of basketball," he sums up.

Victor Wembanyama has said that he wants to "establish the French reign". How do those words make you feel?
I like the fact that he's setting the bar so high for himself and France. I told him he's carrying a unique opportunity for French basketball, which very few players have had in the past. The next Olympics are in Paris. That creates even greater exposure than the NBA can offer him. It's a chance French basketball may have only once in its history, to show that it doesn't just depend on Tony Parker's legacy—which is obviously enormous—but that there's more.

"IF HE MATCHES UP TO EXPECTATIONS, HE COULD JOIN AN ELITE GROUP OF THE MOST FAMOUS PEOPLE IN THE WORLD, NOT JUST IN BASKETBALL."

Victor's strengths are much more than just his size. He's mature beyond his years and already seems ready and confident, with a healthy team around him.

The hype we saw in New York seems unprecedented …
I witnessed the hype surrounding Kobe Bryant, LeBron James, and others. And yet … the difference here is that global access to all kinds of media has reached unprecedented levels, and all you need is a smartphone. Anyone in the world can access Victor Wembanyama clips with just one click. That wasn't the case for Larry Bird, Magic Johnson, Michael Jordan, Kobe, or LeBron. In that sense, what we're seeing is unprecedented. And if he matches up to expectations, he could join an elite group of the most famous people in the world, not just in basketball.

Is it also an opportunity for the NBA?
Yes, it's a huge opportunity for the growth of the NBA. I want to be careful and not overburden him with pressure. But he'll attract a lot of attention. When you see the development of basketball in Africa, his father's background [Democratic Republic of Congo] could further expand the level of interest he's going to generate. In a way he reminds me of Yao Ming. He's a real citizen of the world, like Yao, who had that ability to blend his basketball career with something that went beyond sport. Victor has shared his concerns with us about global water shortages. The NBA is very committed to environmental issues and will give him a platform so he can have an impact on causes he feels are important.

Tony Parker in the Hall of Fame, your meeting with Emmanuel Macron in 2022, NBA games in Paris, the 2024 Olympics—has the NBA ever had a stronger relationship with a country than it does with France right now?
It's one of the strongest relationships. There's a tradition in France. It's not an accident that it's the country with the most foreign players in this league, along with Canada. And it's not just a question of genes but is also down to its scouting and training system. The combination of all these factors will make France an unparalleled stage for the promotion of basketball, both in the country itself and around the world. This could be a turning point for our international growth, which began shortly after I got here in 1992. Back then it was the Barcelona Olympics and the arrival of Michael Jordan. Victor told me that his parents met at those Games. If you believe that certain numbers are magical, it will be interesting to see if the number 92 reappears in his career in some way or other. Our league is becoming more and more international. Nearly a third of our players are from overseas. We've launched the BAL in Africa and discussions are ongoing to increase our activity in Europe and Latin America. Basketball is living through a golden age. 2023 could well be a new turning point for it. ●

CHAPTER 6

Double agents

SINCE THE LATE 1990S, BOUNA NDIAYE AND JÉRÉMY MEDJANA HAVE REACHED A NEW LEVEL. THEIR AGENCY COMSPORT HAS TAKEN VICTOR WEMBANYAMA ALL THE WAY TO THE TOP AND NOW HAS NBA CONTRACTS WORTH CLOSE TO A BILLION DOLLARS.

I t's now only a hop, skip, and a jump from La Grande Borne in France to the Big Apple. Memories of the apartment blocks on the underprivileged housing estate in Grigny (in the *département* of Essonne) where he spent part of his adolescence still come up when 57-year-old player agent Bouna talks about the ultimate prize awarded on June 22. With his lifelong friend Jérémy, aged 51, they planted their flag in New York by leading Victor to the number one pick in the NBA Draft. An adventure started in 1999 by the duo after traveling the world with Slam Nation, an endeavor which teetered on the brink of collapse several times, but was an unprecedented performance for foreigners, and also for an African agent. In short, a new milestone for the agency—the only fully independent non-local agency in the United States—and now an essential player in a market that initially wanted nothing to do with it.

HOW DO YOU FEEL ABOUT YOUR NBA JOURNEY?

Bouna Ndiaye: It's the culmination of three decades of work in a niche that I believe is the most important in world sport, namely France and Africa. It's all our accumulated experience—including failures and players who abandoned us, and then those who trusted us—that makes us the best people to support Victor, to gain his confidence and that of his parents. We took up the challenge from A to Z, in our own way, against the US behemoths. It's a message of

In millions of dollars, the estimated total contract amount for players signed to the NBA by ComSport since their first, D J Mbenga in 2004, including Victor Wembanyama, Bilal Coulibaly, and Rayan Rupert.

great hope to see that with Jérémy and the others I've managed to get here given where I started from. I'm proud to have become an icon—I'm not afraid of the word—like Masai Ujiri, the first African NBA president who led his team to the championship, Joel Embiid, Pascal Siakam and others. Proud to embody a belief that can be duplicated by millions of people: with hard work, you can achieve your biggest dreams.

Jérémy Medjana: We almost lost everything when a player [Ronny Turiaf] left us in 2008 two months before signing a first lucrative contract. We'd made a huge investment over many years, at a time when we didn't have the resources. We ended up filing for bankruptcy. What we're experiencing today makes me realize that if you don't have strong mental resources, you won't survive in this jungle. Nicolas Batum and Ian Mahinmi put their trust in us, and then Evan Fournier and Rudy Gobert. We gradually showed everyone who told us we hadn't "done anything"—no players drafted, no big contract, no max contract, no lottery pick—that we could do it. What would they say to us today? [*Smiles*]

HOW DID YOU FEEL DURING THE DRAFT?

Bouna Ndiaye: The first things that come to me are the shining face of 18-year-old Bilal Coulibaly when his name was called, the difficult wait of Rayan Rupert [43rd], and the emotion of Victor who broke down, something he very rarely does. It was wonderful. I told him: "It makes me happy, I finally get to see you're human!" [*Laughs*] When you enter the green room—the area demarcated for favorites in the first round—you don't have the perspective to savor what brought you to that moment in time.

But I realize now we've done something spectacular, that we may never experience again. There's the Draft, but also what we did around Victor, with the Mets, throughout the year. We impacted French basketball, like the powerhouses of Monaco and ASVEL, by filling Bercy and Roland-Garros. But also world basketball, by affecting hundreds of millions of people thanks to his charisma and the NBA. Respect from others has doubled or even tripled. Even the NBA wasn't talking about the "2023 Draft" but the Wemby Draft. You could also say it was the ComSport Draft. What do I feel today? An indescribable energy, a determination that's stronger than ever to impact others, to help them achieve their dreams, first and foremost, before anything to do with money. It's an obsession.

Jérémy Medjana: Proud. It's an exceptional achievement. For me personally, I'd been supporting him for a long time. It's awesome, as if you were touching the holy grail. Like a player who becomes an NBA champion. For an agent, what could be better? We had our first contact with his family when Victor was 13. There was no question of representing him yet, but we'd seen how special he was. We'd known his mother for a long time, especially Bouna, whose kids had been coached by Élodie [de Fautereau]. But that connection didn't change anything: they were approached by everyone. We had to show we were up to the job. We have that experience, that ability to manage without going through agencies or support agents. We knew how to anticipate what was coming and were never overwhelmed, despite the hurricane that accompanied his emergence and then the explosion in his last season in 2022–2023. It's galvanized us to live through that. ●

The day before the Draft, surrounded by members of the public, journalists, and NYPD security services, Victor Wembanyama donned the jersey of baseball legend Joe DiMaggio and treated himself to a memorable trip to Yankee Stadium on the New York subway.

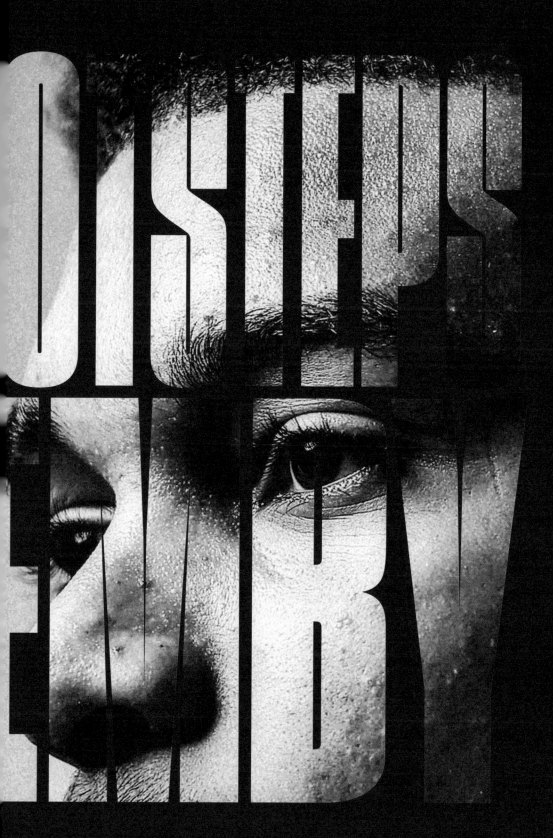

FEET ON THE FLOOR

RUNNING, PUSHING OFF, LANDING JUMPS, RISK OF INJURY—IN BASKETBALL, AND ESPECIALLY FOR VERY TALL PLAYERS, THE FEET ARE FUNDAMENTAL. VICTOR WEMBANYAMA AND HIS TEAM HAVE ALWAYS GIVEN THEM THE METICULOUS ATTENTION THEY DESERVE.

 lawing the floor with the tips of his contracted toes, on all fours, his trunk horizontal but perfectly aligned, he begins to slowly crawl forward. The date is November 11, 2022, in Panevezys. While the Lithuanian team is warming up on the boards, before Victor dons the blue jersey for the first time (20 points, 9 rebounds in the coming win, 90-65), he practices the "bear crawl," a fitness exercise designed to mobilize multiple muscle groups. It is a body movement made spectacular by the sheer size of the player from Le Chesnay, whose pre-game routine is carefully scrutinized by his team. This physical and joint activation exercise makes the feet work especially hard—a core issue. "All basketball players should work on their feet. They absorb impact, restore force, and send elastic energy back to the rest of the body. And each time you jump … you fall back onto them," laughs Guillaume Alquier, Wembanyama's physical trainer, who has developed numerous exercises to support Wemby's feet. Before his matches, Wembanyama can also be seen standing bolt upright as he follows a straight line, moving forward by performing tiny jumps using only the strength of his toes. "The feet are the base of the skeleton. They must be able to withstand impact. If they're not stable, it can create a chain reaction affecting the ankle, leg, knee, hip, and spine. And we know what that can lead to," continues Alquier. "So this part of the body must be powerful, controlled, and balanced." In the case of tall players, this issue is even more crucial, as the slightest lack of precision can become a source of injury.

"We have unrivaled experience in minimizing the risk of injuries and stress fractures. We know how to avoid them with players who have long feet."

BOUNA NDIAYE THE PLAYER'S AGENT

The memory of centers whose careers were badly affected—Bill Walton—or even ruined—Greg Oden—by lower limb injuries is a reminder of how this factor can impact longevity. The American Chet Holmgren and number two pick in the 2022 Draft, whose profile (7ft 1in) has often been compared to that of Wembanyama—whom he faced in the final of the U19 World Cup in 2021—failed to play a single minute in the NBA with Oklahoma City in 2022–2023. His debut had to wait until a full year later.

The reason? A midfoot ligament tear during an exhibition game in August. "A tall player is heavier and will fall from higher," explains Alquier. "So it's more dangerous for a 7ft 4in player who wears 20.5 size shoes like Victor than for a 5ft 9in playmaker."

"We have unrivaled experience in minimizing the risk of injuries and stress fractures. We know how to avoid them with players who have long feet," explains Bouna Ndiaye. "Our experience and expertise with players of this profile over several decades has helped us create a specially tailored program for Victor over the past three years. We focus on his body to make it safer, using a different approach."

For Victor Wembanyama, it's also an obsession that dates back to childhood and his first steps in the sport. His father, Félix, a former triple jumper and long jumper who could run 100 meters in 11 seconds, made sure he never put a foot wrong. "As a former elite athlete, he instinctively corrected me and told me if my foot was making a strange movement," Wembanyama explained to us during two interviews in September 2021 and February 2022. "You have to learn to run the right way, especially with my height and build. Even if you're gifted with great motor skills and fluidity of movement, you can't just make running technique up. It's not easy and I'm nowhere near mastering it all. It's hard work and underestimated. We also practiced athletics and running several times over the summer. I was 11 and my sister Ève was just entering the training academy. The results of those intense sessions can still be seen today."

The sessions continued in a different form at the Mets with Alquier. The player's personal trainer uses spiky massage balls, plates, and other accessories to create "sensory input" and stimulate the neurological connections between Wembanyama's brain and his pedal extremities. The aim is to develop the "intrinsic and extrinsic" muscles that come into play when using the feet, and take them out of their comfort zone to produce better reactions in dangerous situations. It's not unusual, for example, to see the 7ft 4in Wemby lean on his ankle when twisted at a right angle and perform a few jumps. "We want to approximate the

With Geoffrey Wandji, doctor of the French national team (left), and Manuel Lacroix, physical trainer of ASVEL and the French team.

injury in movement so the body learns to understand it better," explains Alquier. "It's about habituating the tissues by working at ranges bordering on the extreme and, from there, creating the strength to know how to react. Proprioception isn't about standing on an inflatable balance board and waiting! [*Laughs*] It's about knowing the position of your body in space. Balance is good for activating the muscles, but that's not enough.

Walking barefoot, for example, is helpful. I was always told it was dangerous in the weights room, but I think the opposite. The benefits outweigh the risks of a weight falling on the feet. I'd love it if Victor could walk barefoot on the lawn at home, but he lives in an apartment. [*Laughs*] The goal of all this is to proactively create motor control over the greatest possible range of movement." So that he always ends up … landing on his feet. ●

★ WHAT WEMBY SAYS ★

"The feet are an important factor. You have to learn to run the right way, especially with my height and build. Even if you're gifted with great motor skills and fluidity of movement, you can't just make running technique up. It's not easy and I'm nowhere near mastering it all. It's hard work and underestimated. In that sense, my father played an essential role as a former elite athlete who did the triple jump, the long jump, and ran the 100 meters in 11 seconds. He always instinctively corrected me and told me if my foot was making a strange movement. We also practiced athletics and running several times over the summer. I was 11. The result of those intense sessions can still be seen today."

Film

THE CALL OF THE NORTH

IT WAS DURING AN INFORMAL U11 WORLD CUP TOURNAMENT IN BOURBOURG, NEAR GRAVELINES, IN THE NORTH OF FRANCE, THAT VICTOR WEMBANYAMA WAS FIRST SPOTTED BY TALENT SCOUTS. HE WAS JUST TEN YEARS OLD.

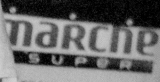

BOURBOURG (in the *département* of Nord)—The sparkling disco ball throws its reflections onto the wooden slats lining the ceiling of the Albert Denvers sports hall, named after a socialist politician born in Gravelines. Hanging from the ceiling of the Bourbourg venue, the flags of France, Italy, Germany, and Lithuania flutter gently, moving to the vibrations of the sound system. With a DJ at the helm, it pumps out mainstream hits while the last tense minutes of a basketball game play out on the boards. The players are only ten years old but look like they are playing the game of their lives.

Welcome to the Mini-Basketball World Cup (under 11s) taking place on this Easter weekend of 2023. The event has acquired a growing international reputation during the 30 years it has been held in the small town of Bourbourg (population 7,100). But it unexpectedly fell under the spotlight thanks to one of its former participants: Victor Wembanyama. It was back in 2014 and 2015, when the prodigy was still taking his first steps with Nanterre. Today, people are still talking about him.

"Yes, yes, he took part, he was here," we hear around the edges of the court in the modest but crowded stands, taken over by the families, friends, and acquaintances of the 240 competitors, divided into 24 teams from a variety of clubs: the French LNB league including Nanterre, the title holders, Le Portel and Gravelines; European outfits such as Alba Berlin and Zalgiris Kaunas; and those from other horizons like the "Travel Team" made up of Lithuanian and Ukrainian players. The weekend's festivities include basketball, entertainment, dance, a slam dunk and three-pointer competition, as well as a sound and light show. Just like the grownups.

"It's more than a tournament," say the organizers about this competition—the local club plays at pre-national level—created for the long haul in tribute to a former player, Bernard Kiers, who died during a match in 1988 after a ruptured aneurysm.

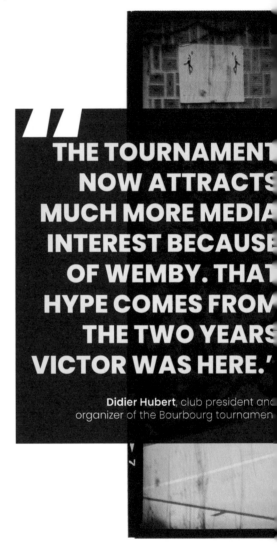

"THE TOURNAMENT NOW ATTRACTS MUCH MORE MEDIA INTEREST BECAUSE OF WEMBY. THAT HYPE COMES FROM THE TWO YEARS VICTOR WAS HERE."

Didier Hubert, club president and organizer of the Bourbourg tournament

"All the kids know that Victor played here and that really motivates them," says Klym Artamonov, Ukrainian point guard of Loon Plage (N1 division) and assistant coach of the "Travel Team" which won the 2023 edition. "The tournament now attracts more media interest because of Wemby," says Didier Hubert, club president and organizer. "We've had dozens more registration requests. That hype comes from the two years Victor was here. He was tall, smiley, charming, and

had a sense of fair play. He dribbled and dunked in a game, which was rare. Those images left their mark on us. He himself is proud to talk about his memories from here. The kids, who follow the NBA, inevitably imagine at some point that they're in his shoes." When people first met the beanpole of a boy with his nonstop smile, many initially took him for a big brother, or even for the coach of Nanterre. In fact, Wembanyama was going through a trial period at that point.

Spotted at a run-of-the-mill game by Michaël Alard (the man who discovered him), he had left his club Entente Le Chesnay-Versailles after a first but not hugely memorable experience, and was thinking about where he should settle to continue his apprenticeship.

The Bourbourg experience was not insignificant in his decision to set up home in the French *département* of Hauts-de-Seine. "It was a pivotal moment," says Frédéric Donnadieu, current president of

Nanterre 92, who at that time gave up his role of assistant coach on the pro bench where he supported his brother Pascal on the EuroLeague courts, to take charge of the U11s in the club. "Even for me, who'd watched many tournaments, it was unique, with CSKA Moscow, Berlin, and so on, an incredible level of play, and a highly intense and moving experience for the kids. At that age, you can already sense the depth in certain people. There are some things that are innate, and there was something about Victor that was already obvious—his competitive nature, his way of playing. At the time, I already let

him lay the ball up, dribble it between his legs, do stuff behind his back. There was no way I was going to just leave him under the basket. He did lose his fair share of balls. [Laughs] But he brought a new dynamic and positive energy to the whole group. It was exciting for all the kids. He was already a mini-star. When we lost the final in 2014, everyone was devastated, in tears." In 2015, Nanterre emerged triumphant and won the final thanks to the slam dunks of its new outstanding player. "In that category, there's nothing comparable anywhere in the world," Wembanyama told us in September 2021.

"I CAN STILL SEE HIM IN THE DORMITORY, HIS LONG BODY WRITHING ON THE FLOOR, PRETENDING TO BE A CATERPILLAR."

Pierre Molenat, teammate of Wemby in 2015

"It was a great first experience at a high level for that age. It's not where I realized I wanted to go pro, but it was a lot of fun."

HIS FIRST TITLE

Also present in Bourbourg in 2014 and 2015 were Kymany Houinsou (ex-ASVEL) and Sidy Cissoko, one of Wemby's youth rivals, and now his teammate in San Antonio with the Spurs in the NBA. For those who witnessed his presence, the friendly and warm personality of the still-rough diamond had as much impact on them as his height. "He was very normal," recalls Pierre Molenat, his teammate in 2015. "The media wasn't yet all over him, he was a kid in his head. He loved to laugh and wind us up. After the second night, we'd won everything and I can still see him in the dormitory, his long body writhing on the floor, pretending to be a caterpillar. [*Laughs*] More than the win, those are the things that stay with you: our life as a team, the jokes before bed, the meals we shared. It's for life."

But that did not stop Wembanyama from starting to shape himself as a basketball player and to assert his identity as a competitor. "When I talked to him about it again, the first thing he told me, without any arrogance but a touch of childish frustration, was that they hadn't named him MVP," smiles Fred Sourice, a journalist at La Voix du Nord which had covered the event. "There wasn't yet a huge amount of hype around him. Of course, it's hard to predict the future, but seeing him aged 10 or 11 with such dexterity, a child in a 6ft 2in body, I did wonder what he might become."

Kevin Donnadieu, son of Pascal and assistant coach to Frédéric at Bourbourg, adds: "He was already charismatic and unusual. The kids were all looking at him, he was signing autographs. His very first move, with Nathan Zulemie [who also trained at Nanterre], finished with an alley-oop. He won his first title here [in 2015], and even if you're relatively carefree at that age, you don't forget it. And yet, what stays with me, more than the basketball itself, is his warmth and kindness. He was natural, joyful. He wasn't thinking about how far he could go."

But others were thinking of it for him. The most fanatical US scouts, or at least those who had access to Nanterre, were already aware, back in 2015, that an 11-year-old prospect had stood out in a town in northern France, and were starting to build an image bank, videos, and reports on Wembanyama. ●

Destiny in his

DRAWING, LEGO, RELENTLESS TECHNICAL WORK SIN
HIS TEENS—HOW VICTOR WEMBANYAMA TURNED H
ENORMOUS HANDS, WHICH COULD HAVE BEEN A LIABILIT
IN THE ELITE GAME, INTO AN UNDISPUTED WEAPO

own hands

Karim Boubekri

H is long finger bones must surely remember the contact of burning leather under the scorching August sun, and the thousands of crossovers, dribbles, shots, and running steps on the crimson asphalt of the streetball court adjoining the Paul Vaillant-Couturier sports complex. It was here that Karim Boubekri organized training sessions for U13s. It was renovated in 2018 with surrounding trees and solar panels which now cover the space that is designated for the youth of Nanterre. The passionate coach formed and forged in Choisy-le-Roi describes it at the time as a "run-down little playground" where some sections have been damaged and come loose over the years, but this was the spot where Victor laid the foundations for the ball-in-hand dexterity that is creating havoc today.

It was here that he transformed what could (or should?) have been a liability for a player of his size into a strength.

Crossover and behind-the-back dribbles, spin shots, backward shots, one-legged three-pointers, head-at-the-rim slam dunks, and surreal blocks where he places his hand like a lid over the attempts of the opposition: the range of moves available to the young man who grew up near the Palace of Versailles appears to be unlimited. It has taken him years to refine their subtleties.

"In theory, the bigger your hands are, the harder it is to shoot," explained Wembanyama during two interviews in September 2021 and February 2022. "But you should also see it as an advantage: you can catch the ball with ease, go for a dunk faster and more easily … This skill I have is a talent that was given to me, it feels like a gift, something innate. But to get the most out of it, you have to cultivate it every day. When I was very young, I worked on dribbling with two balls, and lots of other stuff like that. I always wanted to play in the NBA. But the clearcut drive, the awareness that I was ready to do what it would take to get there dates back to those U12, U13 years at Nanterre. Karim was my first coach who focused on individual work and technique. With him I learned what it was like to work super-hard on myself."

In the morning, the youngsters arrive "with their bottle of water, jump rope, and gloves," says the man who cut his coaching teeth in Charenton, crossing paths with Evan Fournier, Lahaou Konaté, and Jérémy Nzeulie. Gloves? "To work on their handles without the sensitivity that your fingers give you. I saw it in an interview with White Chocolate—former Sacramento point guard Jason Williams. At first, you're all over the place, you don't know where the ball is, you have to dribble harder. Then when you take them off, your senses and abilities are unleashed. You fly with the ball."

This is just one idea among many adopted by this enthusiast of individual development and an expert in the crossover dribble. Sometimes, the teenagers have to handle the orange sphere wrapped in a plastic bag, "a Kyrie Irving thing that he did as a youngster with his dad." Some balls are weighted.

There's no limit to the body of moves, each of which can be repeated up to 250 times in a morning.

"You mix fakes, footwork, speed of execution, dribbling hand, you combine stuff together …" explains Boubekri. Among the classics, the coach teaches the "killer crossover" of Tim Hardaway, that of Allen Iverson, and even "El Latigo," the signature dribble of Dejan Bodiroga also known as the "Shammgod."

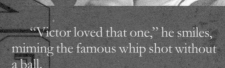

"Victor loved that one," he smiles, miming the famous whip shot without a ball.

A child of the 80s and 90s, Boubekri learned his craft on asphalt courts to the sound of ghetto blasters, with Hammadoun Sidibé, founder of the Quai 54 tournament, and grew up worshipping US basketball in the era of French magazine *5 Majeur* and its focus on the American game, Michael Jordan, and the Dream Team of Barcelona. He drew his inspiration from the rare VHS videos doing the rounds at the time—the documentary *Come Fly with Me* on MJ, and the movie *The Pistol: The Birth of a Legend*, which tells the story of Pete Maravich, an expert in the around-the-body pass in the 1970s. He later used the mixtapes of the brand AND1 for freestyle inspiration.

"There was no YouTube at the time," smiles Boubekri. "When we came across a sequence where Magic Johnson was

Dejan Bodiroga

SHAMMGOD

Pete Maravich in 1988. ©Getty Images

65

"

You often get shorter players who want to challenge the giants. With Victor, it was the opposite, a big man who wants to mix it up with the short guys. We made him work exactly like the point guards. With his high center of gravity, he had to do more than the others to adapt-be precise on dribbles, bend over more, move wider on fakes. He liked to try out new things and trick the opponent with a cross or an unpredictable pass. "

Karim Boubekri

dribbling on a bike, or we saw Maravich blindfolded and dribbling the ball on top of train tracks, it was a window to another world. We were fascinated, and that's all we did for weeks."

A big fan of martial arts—the movies of Jackie Chan—and Japanese animation—*Dragon Ball*, *Saint Seiya*—he brings the values of hard work and resilience they portray into his training. He likes to call places such as the Nanterre court, where he puts his young protégés through brutal sessions, "The Time Chamber"—in *Dragon Ball*, a place where one year of training is equivalent to three years of work.

He does everything he can to ensure that his drills are both fun and challenging.

Boubekri's methods and pop culture references appeal to Victor. Even as a kid, he hated being categorized as a "big" and was just as keen to develop his ability to play guard. He understood enough about the importance of working with his hands to convince his future coaches not to condemn him to standing in the paint with his arms raised.

"You often get shorter players who want to challenge the giants. With Victor, it was the opposite, a big man who wants to mix it up with the short guys," says Boubekri. "We made him work exactly like the point guards. With his high center of gravity, he had to do more than the others to adapt—be precise on dribbles, bend over more, move wider on fakes.

He liked to try out new things and trick the opponent with a cross or an unpredictable pass."

The results of this long-term work are telling, not only in his shot work and handles but also in terms of his stats. In his last pro season before the USA in 2022–2023, Wembanyama made 82.8 percent of his free throws. An extremely rare percentage for a big man, in an exercise that requires perfect coordination and control of his ten fingers—positioning, flick of the wrist, and ball release. Nikola Jokić, double NBA MVP and 2023 champion with Denver, has a similar career success rate of 82.9 percent.

Victor's current physical trainer, Guillaume Alquier, is part of the reason

his stats are so good. His routines include a number of exercises focused on this part of the body—including juggling and use of sensory massage balls—to hone motor and neurological capacity. For example, Wemby has already been witnessed spinning three basketballs in the air in training. "He has a good understanding of his body in space and likes to stimulate that type of fine motor skill," says Alquier. "Certain things affect the muscles, brain, hand-eye coordination, and so on."

Wembanyama is constantly "activating" his hands. He looks after them in many different ways. An occasional cook for his family or himself, he would shop at the market near the Île de la Jatte lying at the boundary between Neuilly and Levallois, where he lived during his year with Metropolitans 92. There was always room in his basket for mangoes, clementines, and grapes.

Another "digital" attraction is building bricks, a passion which had not escaped the staff at San Antonio. When he arrived at the AT&T Center on the day after the Draft, the Spurs had placed a big Eiffel Tower made of LEGO next to the podium set up for Wemby's first press conference.

His love of the bricks started out as a family affair. "I'm crazy about *Star Wars*," he says. "I watched all the movies with my dad. And from the age of four, I started building LEGO models from that world. It's a wholesome activity and requires a lot of precision. It relaxes me but still gets my head and hands working, and I like that. Just like drawing.'

Mad about drawing since childhood, Wembanyama picks up a pencil whenever he can. "I listened in class, but as soon as I had 30 seconds, I'd draw something," he says. "Regular, run-of-the-mill things.

"It's true that in theory, the bigger your hands are, the harder it is to shoot. But you should also see it as an advantage: you can catch the ball with more ease, go for a dunk more easily... This skill I have is a talent that was given to me, it feels like a gift, something innate. But to get the most out of it, you have to cultivate it every day."

A face, a monster, an animal," with enough precision, however, to astound his team-mates and friends and family.

"I used to see him drawing on the team bus," says Alquier. "That definitely helped him. You engage the brain and that does something. LEGO activates something else. By extension, all that work has an effect on the court."

"They're never characters that already exist. I don't like to copy or imitate. I want to create and invent," continues Wembanyama in an uncanny parallel with the creativity he's developing on the court. "They're just quick sketches; it's been a long time since I sat down for an hour to draw. It's a talent that runs in the family, with my mother studying architecture. I don't want to sell pictures; I just like telling a story.

One day I'll really focus on it and work on my technique and all the rest. The plot? It's a secret, but I already have the story in my head. I'll draw it one day," he promises. And then concludes by saying: "I've got other things to accomplish first." ●

"I'm crazy about *Star Wars*. I watched all the movies with my dad. And from the age of four, I started building LEGO models from that world. It's a wholesome activity and requires a lot of precision. It relaxes me but still gets my head and hands working, and I like that. Just like drawing."

GREEN BLOOD IN HIS VEINS

HIS FAME WENT GLOBAL WITH THE METS. BUT BEFORE BOULOGNE AND ASVEL,
IT WAS IN NANTERRE, FROM THE AGE OF TEN TO SEVENTEEN,
THAT VICTOR WEMBANYAMA REFINED AND CEMENTED HIS VOCATION.
AND WHERE HE LAID THE FOUNDATIONS OF HIS FUTURE DESTINY.

The buzzer sounds. Instead of heading down the tunnel of the Maurice-Thorez arena in Nanterre like his Mets teammates, Victor rushes toward the stands. Carried away by a powerful wave of emotion and guided by instinct, he gives himself up to the delirious crowd who scream their love for him while uncontrolled tears pour from his eyes and the child within returns to his face.

It's almost as if the blue of his Metropolitans jersey turns to green, and the 92 of Boulogne fades away to reveal the 32 he wore with his favorite club. On this day of May 9, 2023, a week before the NBA Draft Lottery, the young "big" from Boulogne-Levallois cuts the cord. He has just inflicted defeat on his first pro club (82-72), controlling the game with impressive authority (25 points, 17 rebounds, 4 blocks).

Instead of celebrating the win, Wembanyama parties with the people who shaped him from the age of ten until his departure for ASVEL, just before he came of age in 2021.

This is the first time since he left the club that he has returned to the court, an injury when he came back with ASVEL the previous year keeping him on the bench. It's also the last before his departure for the USA. So the hugs continue, with Frédéric Donnadieu (president and former coach), Vincent Dziagwa (physical trainer), Philippe Da Silva (pro assistant), Michaël Alard (the man who discovered him), and Pascal Donnadieu.

"It really floored us to see him express himself like that," says Alard. "That moment will stay in my memory forever," adds Pascal Donnadieu, who launched Wemby in the Betclic Élite pro league and the EuroCup before he turned 16. "I'm normally pretty restrained, so to see that emotion and spontaneity from a young man we've supported for so long was the greatest gift he could give us. It shows who he is as a person. I was the last person in the line if you like. But lots of people invested their time and energy in the club around him. It's a privilege to have been able to help him get to where he is today.

Wembanyama, nicknamed "the alien" by LeBron James, has green blood in his veins. "Green's a color I really like," he said at the Draft. The shade of his suit on the red carpet at the Barclays Center in Brooklyn on June 22, 2023, was as much a nod to his Hauts-de-Seine club as his "extraterrestrial" affiliation.

During his last year in France, we met him several times in Levallois, leaving the weights room or individual sessions, with his Nanterre jersey on his shoulders. The framed version given to him by the club sat prominently in the living room of his apartment in Lyon, between vintage posters of Marvel comic books and LEGO models in display cases.

Frédéric Donnadieu

The bond started to form one day in 2014, when Michaël Alard, on seeing the beanpole boy from Entente Le Chesnay-Versailles, mistook him for a member of staff from the opposing team.

"I was coaching an U13 regional game," explains Alard, who has been a card-carrying member of JSF Nanterre since the age of five. "He was playing in the U10s, and when I realize he's a player, my eyes light up. A player's father, Freddy Kabala, nudges me [*laughs*] and says he knows the dad. Two minutes later, I was chatting with Félix [Wembanyama]. I immediately saw there was something special about this tall, lanky kid. The Bourbourg tournament [U11 World Cup in the French *département* of Nord] was happening a few months later. I suggested he come and train with us on Wednesdays."

The young Victor attends diligently and becomes a registered member of the club the following summer. A relationship of trust is built with his parents, Félix and Élodie, who do everything they can to protect their son from the attention he is getting from all corners of the globe once he hits 13. "He played his first U15 game, outperforming as usual," remembers Frédéric Donnadieu, current president of Nanterre, who became a close friend of the family and was invited to New York to attend the Draft. "I see a guy take his phone out and start filming him warming up. I go down and angrily tell him to stop. His agent Jérémy tells me it's Mike Schmitz, the ESPN scout specialist. Already! There'd been interest before that, but it was more low-key. The Île-de-France training center tried to get him to move there, but he preferred to stay here. From his first junior year in France, French scouts representing

> " **It was his first U15 game and I see a guy take out his phone and start filming him. I go down and angrily tell him to stop. It was Mike Schmitz, the scout specialist from ESPN.**"
>
> Frédéric Donnadieu

"The reason I love this club so much is because it fits with who I am and who my parents are, and with my philosophy. They supported me in my plans and ambitions, put in place what I needed to go higher. As well as upgrading me to the next age category each year, when I said I wanted to work more or needed adjustments, they always did their best. It was very hard to leave and that's how it should be. It was a bit like leaving home."

the NBA franchises were around. Félix and Élodie asked us to do a bit of policing. I've never seen that at that age before. Tony Parker didn't have that. He's set a precedent."

When it comes to his training, Nanterre have the intelligence to embrace Wembanyama's unusual profile. "A big guy who wants to rub shoulders with the little guys," sums up Karim Boubekri nicely, a specialist in dribbling and individual technical work who retains a special place in the player's heart. Alard and Frédéric Donnadieu give him the freedom to express his creativity, his love of runs, three-pointers, and blind passes. "There was no question of making him play 'like an adult,'" explains Donnadieu. "I made him do drills with two balls, things that were advanced

for his age. He made mistakes and lost lots of balls in the beginning. We had to find the right balance between correcting him and treating him like anyone else, but without restricting him. He doesn't necessarily realize it, but it's not always easy for coaches." [*Laughs*]

The values of humility and hard work advocated by the Hauts-de-Seine club are in perfect sync with his upbringing. He takes up residence in a studio apartment on the second floor of the Chanzy apartment building near the club's arena. His name is still displayed on a plaque there. He spends long periods of time alone, shunning screens and preferring to read or draw. The club buys him a larger bed so he can sleep without his feet hanging off the end.

An unprecedented team is set up around Wembanyama. In addition to meticulous physical training with Vincent Dziagwa, Victor benefits from personalized sessions with Michaël Bur (young prospects), Jessy Valet (U18s), Philippe Da Silva, Amine El Hajraoui (France juniors assistant and dorm supervisor). They also have to remember to give priority to his academic objective of the baccalaureate, which he passes a year early.

Progress is rapid, consistent, and astonishing. But above and beyond all that, everyone remembers his charisma. Wembanyama is unanimously praised for his likable personality, his smile, and extraordinary maturity, coupled with his love of the game and the group, which is as rare as his ability to raise his game when the pressure ramps up and to pull others along behind him.

"When a kid's ten years old, it's unhealthy to think about the future," says Frédéric Donnadieu. "But I pretty quickly realized that unless he lost his love of the game, or girls or other distractions took him away from it, he would be unique. What he's achieving today is what he was already doing in the decisive moments in the Final Four at Tain L'Hermitage where we ended up as undefeated French U15 champions."

Bryan George, who guided Wembanyama that year, has never forgotten it. "His first basket in the regional U15s is a Klay Thompson type move," smiles the video coordinator of the French national team and the Atlanta Hawks. "He runs coast to coast on the side—a strange sight as he wasn't yet as skilled as he is today. He receivesthe ball on the move and shoots a three. I was like, 'Is he crazy?' And then … swish. So then I think: who am I to tell him what he can or can't do, if he feels it, is having fun, and his teammates accept it? It was one of his gifts. Imposing his way of doing things without being demanding, convincing others with his kindness. He has a deep connection with Nanterre. The period from 12 to 15 is pivotal, it's where you shape your personality.

"He impacted the club and the generations around him. In an ultracompetitive environment, he showed you could do it without being a jerk. It's extremely rare. And if I take away all the basketball stuff, Victor blew my mind. It was an encounter that changed me."

"An artist," adds Michaël Alard. "On the court, it's as if he was painting. He's creative and expresses his emotions with the competitiveness of a top athlete and the carefree attitude of a kid doing it for fun. He was a boy 6ft 2in tall playing with these hulking guys, making passes behind his back, and even when picked off he somehow managed to get what he wanted, whether he was blocking, going to the basket, or shooting. Victor is a guy with no age and no position. He's stirring things up big time, revolutionizing the game."

The machine is up and running. Once Wembanyama becomes a regular member of the pro team roster from late April 2021, Wemby hardly loses anymore and Nanterre does not lose another game.

[HE'S] AN ARTIST. ON THE COURT, IT'S AS IF HE WAS PAINTING. HE'S CREATIVE AND EXPRESSES HIS EMOTIONS WITH THE COMPETITIVENESS OF A TOP ATHLETE AND THE CAREFREE ATTITUDE OF A KID DOING IT FOR FUN."

Michaël Alard

The announcement of his departure for ASVEL and the EuroLeague a few weeks later is a terrible blow.

"Horrible," remembers Frédéric Donnadieu. "I found out on the night of my birthday. I was depressed for a week. I thought he'd stay for at least another year." The player contacts his first coach directly so he can look him in the eye as he tells him his decision. No parents, no agents, just the two men. The discussion is brief and emotional, on both sides. "He was in tears," continues Donnadieu. "I wasn't going to torture him. It was a tough blow, but I tried not to show it. I didn't hold it against him. But I was realizing that the dream I had of leading a kid from the U11s to the NBA Draft wasn't going to come true. It took me a while to get over it, but by the Fall I was feeling better. We saw each other when he came back with ASVEL. We spoke for two hours face to face and he explained his need for adversity and his desire to play in the EuroLeague. We could only respect his choice, just as we did with his decision not to come back here and go to the Mets with Vincent Collet for the last phase of his training before the NBA."

"The only regret," adds his brother Pascal Donnadieu, "is that the merger on the cards for a while between the Mets and Nanterre never took place, as we could have then worked with both Vincent and Victor."

Two years after the trauma, Victor offered his second family the most beautiful of goodbyes, while leaving hope and a promise behind him: that, if the opportunity presents itself at the end of his career, he will wear the green 32 jersey again. ●

ALQUIER, GUARDIAN OF THE TREASURE

AN INSIGHT INTO THE SECRETS OF PHYSICAL TRAINER GUILLAUME ALQUIER, WHO WON THE TRUST OF VICTOR WEMBANYAMA TO LOOK AFTER HIS MOST PRECIOUS ASSET: HIS BODY.

When this member of staff walked into the cramped Metropolitans 92 weights room with its peeling walls and polished concrete floor in the basement of the Marcel-Cerdan sports arena, an unexpected vision met his eyes. Guillaume Alquier, the physical trainer of the team—and Victor's personal trainer—head pointing downward and toes stretched toward the ceiling, is slaloming on his hands between the orange tatami mats.

"What on earth are you up to, Guillaume?" The answer comes from Wembanyama who is pumping iron not far away. "It's you who should be asking yourself why you don't walk on your hands," laughs the Boulogne-Levallois big man.

It's a snapshot that sums up why Wemby and Alquier have formed an unbreakable bond in less than a year. Both men like to think upside down and back to front. "The handstand and walking on your hands in a workout interests me because it activates your vestibular system, the inner ear, as well as working your muscles. I like that about Victor. He's curious and wants to explore as much as possible, to understand the 'why' behind things. He brings amazing agency to his plans," says the native of Clermont, who from age 7 to 11 lived in Kourou, French Guiana, a sparsely populated area on the South American Atlantic coast, famous for its spaceport which has been launching Ariane rockets since the 1960s.

Returning to mainland France, Alquier settled in the *département* of Pyrénées-Atlantiques near Tarbes, completing a sports science degree and a master's in physical and psychological conditioning. He cut his teeth between Oloron-Sainte-Marie and Pau, where he simultaneously managed a third division rugby team and the youth setup of the basketball club Élan Béarnais.

With the Pau pro team from 2017 to 2022 before joining the Mets for the 2022–2023 season with Boulogne-Levallois Metropolitans 92, and a regular at Tony Parker's summer camps, he's now working to put another type of spacecraft into orbit.

He is chief engineer of one of the most important and sensitive missions related to Victor Wembanyama: managing his physical preparation and the development of his body. It's the foundation of everything else, for a frame (7ft 4in) that many consider to be at greater risk of injury than shorter mortals.

"For me, he's a human being like any other. I would say he's more developed than many of us from a motor skills point of view. We do core exercises that are known to be difficult for tall guys, which he does better and for longer than the playmakers. When I tell him it should be hard, he smiles and assures me it's nothing of the sort. And he goes ahead and does it. Victor likes playing with this stuff, the challenge of it."

> "For me, he's a human being like any other. I would say he's more developed than many of us from a motor skills point of view."

It's another reason they are a good match. Alquier's method, which includes a day off a week and regular twice-daily training sessions, has always put fun at the center of things.

Passionate about books and podcasts on his specialties to enhance his toolkit, he might be seen slipping a Rubik's Cube into a player's hand during his recovery time in the weights room. During his pre-game routine, which has become a 13-minute must-watch for spectators and the curious, Wembanyama can be seen rolling spiky massage balls under the arch of his foot, juggling three tennis balls or performing the famous "bear crawl," as well as other unusual drills, in an approach that the man from Pau likes to describe as "holistic"—where the theme or a certain type of training is only one part of the whole. "Lifting weights for the sake of lifting them doesn't interest us," he says. "You have to think beyond the weightlifting mindset where that's all you focus on. I'm interested in neurology, psychomotor functions, coaches who specialize in movement and anyone who does things 'out of the box.'" Juggling may be good, but what does it add and how does it show up in performance? "The more you know how to activate your body in different situations, the better you can be on court."

The menu includes rolling on judo tatami mats as well as sessions in the sand, trampoline park, and pool... but not for swimming. "To understand the element [of water]," explains Alquier. "We'll roll and do somersaults in the water, so the tendons and ligaments are confronted with something else. The aim isn't to play the clown every day. But that shouldn't stop us from making it fun and stepping outside of routines to keep athletes stimulated. Victor responds to it really well."

Emphasis is also placed on "invisible training" such as hydration, nutrition (five meals a day), and sleep (a recommended nine hours a night).

"When you focus only on pure training, you forget the importance of everything else.

For young players who have to work really hard, and therefore recover hard, that's not insignificant. Victor doesn't have his phone in the bedroom, for example," explains Alquier, who prefers to do without high-tech measuring gadgets, such as rings and sensors, favoring a more empirical method to protect his disciple from radio waves.

For a player whose future is under such close scrutiny, establishing guiding principles and a development program is both about meticulous attention to detail and getting the balance right, and Alquier has done the job brilliantly. He began by talking to all the people who helped shape Wemby: his parents Félix (ex-triple jumper and long jumper) and Élodie (ex-basketball player then coach and now a myofascial therapist); physical trainers Vincent Dziagwa (Nanterre) and Manuel Lacroix (ASVEL); his osteopath Patrick Basset; his individual basketball coach Tim Martin; his agents Bouna and Jérémy; and his podiatrist.

"You hear a variety of different opinions about Victor. Firstly, I had to talk to him,"

explains Alquier, whose first meeting with Wembanyama was on August 14, 2022. It was the day before a highly publicized exhibition game played in Nanterre between a selection of French talents—including Bilal Coulibaly, still unknown to the general public, and Oscar Wembanyama, Victor's younger brother—and the high school team of Bronny James, LeBron's son. The physical trainer had been recommended by ComSport, whose leaders were satisfied with the work and results achieved with his Pau players, such as Petr Cornelie and Giovan Oniangue. A first three-hour meeting allowed the trainer to retrace the physical history of the player from Le Chesnay and to let Wembanyama express his vision and personal goals. Alquier was blown away by his determination and maturity. "As I discovered later, he was already ahead of others in terms of knowledge, in terms of understanding. When lifting weights, for example, he's super-precise about his posture, the positioning of his hands and feet. He listens and takes everything in really quickly." There is still, however, much to do.

" I'm interested in neurology, psychomotor functions, coaches who specialize in movement and anyone who does things 'out of the box.' "

but he's now around 229lb [as of April 2023]. But the reality is he doesn't get injured that much." A statement proven by his last French season (2022–2023), where Wembanyama crushed the French championship in terms of stats without missing a Mets game, while posting the most playing time in the division (32.1 minutes), despite the systematic preferential treatment dished out by his opponents. When faced with the ultraphysical defense of ASVEL's Charles Kahudi and Monaco's John Brown in the Playoffs, Wemby, who sometimes bent but never broke, is not the fragile beanpole who some promised would be seriously shocked by the world of the NBA. "In Europe, you can be much more physical than in the US, where a lot of what we do here would be considered a foul," says Mike James, the Monaco superstar. "The NBA game will be to his advantage; he'll have more freedom. He's not yet the finished article from a physical point of view. He'll get faster and stronger. When he reaches his peak, in the right game system, he'll probably be able to do whatever he likes."

The choice of the Mets allowed Wembanyama to optimize his individual development and recovery by dispensing with the travel connected with the EuroCup, and therefore avoid his experience at ASVEL the previous year (EuroLeague), where a multitude of minor injuries had hindered his progress (broken finger, and injuries to his shoulder blade, and psoas muscle, which deprived him of the French championship final won by his team, and from playing in EuroBasket).

It now seems that nothing can stop that progress. And it will continue in Texas, with Alquier. The guardian of his most precious treasure—his body—is already following in his footsteps in the French national team and has also landed a job on the staff of the San Antonio Spurs. ●

"The priority is increasing the strength of his lower body, so he's powerful enough on his legs to be able to absorb multiple sequences of contact and run while low to the ground," explains Alquier. "The second thing is core strength because without it, you can't exploit your size. And then consistency. But we also have to be careful with his bones, which were still growing at the start of the year. You can't load him like you could a 30-year-old. That could lead to small fractures. So gaining weight has never been a goal. Getting heavier isn't a risk-free process, you have to do it consistently. From a muscular point of view, he's lost fat and gained muscle so we're on the right path. He arrived weighing 220lb,

A CLOSE CALL WITH BARÇA

LIKE OTHER ELITE CLUBS, FC BARCELONA DID EVERYTHING THEY COULD TO SNATCH VICTOR WEMBANYAMA FROM NANTERRE, AFTER ENROLLING HIM IN THE MINI COPA DEL REY IN 2018. ALL IN VAIN.

HUESCA (Spain)—Blue and dark red look good on him. There's no mistaking him from the photos and images taken that weekend in February 2018. It is indeed Victor, aged just 14, an FC Barcelona jersey on his back, straight-cut hair and a little smile on his lips as he imperiously and endlessly blocks the attempted shots of a kid from Badalona who does not yet know who he is dealing with. Outside the Centro Insular de Deportes, the former arena of the Gran Canaria club whose yellow seats remain largely empty, early spring sunshine has arrived in the city of Las Palmas where the Mini King's Cup, the junior version of the Copa del Rey, is taking place.

How did the teen from Le Chesnay, who was still a registered member of Nanterre at the time, end up here? In this competition showcasing young talent from the Spanish training academies—the first edition of which in 2004 named a certain Ricky Rubio MVP (European champion in 2009 and 2011, 2019 world champion with La Roja and silver medalist in the 2008 Olympic final against Team USA in Beijing)—the clubs are free to expand their rosters with "guests" from the rest of the continent.

Wembanyama quickly found himself at the top of Ruben Alcaraz's list. After several unsuccessful attempts, Barcelona's director of scouting gets what he wants. "We'd been following him for over a year," he explains. "I arrive in Barcelona and a contact of mine, a German coach, who had seen Nanterre playing in an U13 tournament, tells me about three players, and one in particular. From the very first videos, I thought 'Wow …'

A CLOSE CALL WITH BARÇA

After seeing just a few frames of the Bourbourg tournament, I spoke about him to the manager of the training academy, La Cantera. I quickly realized we were talking about a 'generational' player who can change the destiny of a team, like Dončić when Real Madrid signed him, or even change the game altogether. He's also the first kid in my career where I could see, even at the age of 13, that there was no doubt about his NBA future. Today I would even say that at his peak he'll be one of its very best players. We contacted his mother, who rejected our approaches for a long time before finally accepting."

The prestige of one of the most powerful clubs in the world, the professionalism, the facilities, the promise of elite sport: there's no shortage of arguments for making the Catalan proposal an offer that cannot be refused. However, as Alcaraz explains, Victor's parents are hesitant. They feel guilty, even, toward Nanterre, the club that first welcomed them.

Bryan George, current assistant coach (video coordinator and player development) at the Atlanta Hawks and the French national team (after doing the same job at ASVEL), and Wemby's coach at the time, says: "His parents are like him, different. Personally, if someone said to me: 'your son is good, come to Barcelona, all expenses paid, five-star hotel,' I think I wouldn't even tell my club [*laughs*], I'd just go for it. It could sound like the opportunity of a career. And they didn't want it … They were happy here. Media coverage and the limelight didn't interest them. When they finally said yes, they were almost apologetic. They said they were going there for the experience, that it gave them a rare opportunity to spend a few days on vacation together, but that they were attached to Nanterre, and it wouldn't change anything. I said to them: 'But, of course. Go for it!'"

In the *département* of Hauts-de-Seine, there are bitter memories of this episode because of the way the player was approached (via his parents), Barça not thinking it necessary

to tell the managers of Nanterre what they were doing. "They only notified me at the last minute to ask me to sign some paperwork," Frédéric Donnadieu, president of Nanterre 92, says bitterly. "I knew they were going to try and turn his head. I sent them an angry email and said their methods were unacceptable, especially as at the time we'd made the EuroLeague. We'd even beaten them at home [71-67 in October 2013 after winning one of the most unexpected French championship titles in history]. We don't think we're better than others, but I think we deserve more respect." Barcelona, of course, is germinating the same idea as all the scouts who ever saw Wembanyama move on a court. Some sources even mention, in Wembanyama's case, offers of sums of money and work for his parents if they had decided to settle in Spain. "I don't know what was offered to him. That wasn't my role," says Ruben Alcaraz. "But we're talking about a family, his parents, his brother Oscar who was still a handball player at the time, his sister Ève, also a basketball player, and a young man for whom we were ready to make an extra effort. In that situation, you're not offering a contract, but a life plan. If he'd signed here, Victor would have revolutionized Barça."

When he turns up in Gran Canaria the fascination he elicits is instant, remembers Carlos Flores, coach at Ibiza in the third division (LEB Plata), and a former coach at the Barça training academy, who managed the outstanding player that week in mid-February. "We just stood there, watching this super-tall kid, still a featherweight, shy, doing things that someone his size isn't supposed to do. In the first drill, he grabs a rebound and goes on the counterattack doing a crossover dribble between his legs. It was different from anything I'd ever seen. A big guy with the mentality of a point guard, capable of running or shooting threes. All without any sense of ego. He loved the game and wanted to share. There was nothing normal about him. It was like a collective hallucination.

"The head of La Cantera says to me: 'Make the most of it. One day you can say you coached him.' After the first session, I joked to them: 'Don't let him go home. Lock him in the locker room, hide the key and don't open it until it's time for training,'" says Flores, laughing. "From the moment he set foot in the Ciudad Deportiva, everyone did everything they could to make him want to stay."

Barça would finish third, thanks in particular to a final game in which the French youngster made his mark: 16 points, 15 rebounds and two decisive defensive moves. But in the end, the Wembanyama camp did not move to Catalonia. True to their word, the player and his parents returned to the Île-de-France.

"Things seemed quite fluid in the discussions with his mother," Flores recalls. "But the path was clear to them. They knew where they wanted to go and how to do it." Another possible answer is that Wembanyama may not have had an entirely satisfactory experience.

He confided in Bryan George on his return: "He explained to me that he really wasn't happy about some things. Using the

"IF HE'D SIGNED HERE, VICTOR WOULD HAVE REVOLUTIONIZED BARÇA."

Ruben Alcaraz, director of scouting at Barça

vocabulary and words of a 14-year-old, he said he felt they hadn't given him any feedback, that they hadn't told him things he was doing wrong, and even that they hadn't shouted about it enough. Not like me, who used to yell at him. [*Laughs*] I took that as a compliment. He came back feeling that they were more interested in trying to keep him than help him grow. I was really amazed he could see things with such maturity and clarity, when you might think at that age he'd be intimidated by the situation. As always with him, he has an unusual take on things." ●

CHAPTER 10

THE SECRETS OF THE "UNICORN"

DURING THE 2021 TO 2022 SEASON, THE ONLY ONE HE SPENT WITH ASVEL, THE MOST SUCCESSFUL CLUB IN THE HISTORY OF THE FRENCH LEAGUE, VICTOR WEMBANYAMA ALLOWED *L'ÉQUIPE* TO FOLLOW IN HIS FOOTSTEPS FOR A WHOLE DAY. AN UNPRECEDENTED WINDOW INTO HIS DAILY AND PRIVATE LIFE WHILE HE DEALT WITH PHYSICAL PROBLEMS SLOWING HIS ASCENT TO THE TOP.

ARTICLE PUBLISHED IN *L'ÉQUIPE* ON FEBRUARY 11, 2022

LYON—It's a basketball player with a super-sharp flat top painted on a pink background, dribbling behind his back and dressed in the style of Wesley Snipes in Ron Shelton's cult movie *White Men Can't Jump*, a neon yellow tank over a green T-shirt and retro Air Jordans on his feet. The canvas, painted by artist Ruben Gérard and bought by his family at the Parisian exhibition *Trajectoire* in December 2021, has pride of place in the middle of Victor's living room in Lyon, next to a black clock with immobile hands.

"I've never bothered changing the batteries," laughs the new ASVEL star, already relatively busy as he relaunches a season on hold since December 15, 2021, because of a minor shoulder blade injury picked up in a loss to Saint Petersburg in the EuroLeague. Wembanyama would make a return to the EuroLeague courts against Panathinaikos on February 11, 2022, (63-76 defeat, 5 points and 5 rebounds in 14 minutes). A week earlier, the power forward of the French champions, at that time still measuring 7ft 2in at age 18, took advantage of a rare moment of calm in an overloaded and minutely orchestrated schedule—even his visits to the medical room are timed—to generously open the doors of his home to *L'Équipe*. With his teammates away in Turkey for two European games, he was completing his preparations for returning to the game.

His face had disappeared from team photos in recent weeks, as had his name from the stats sheets. But if you had hung around the greenhouses of Lyon's Tête d'Or park, or taken a sneak peek at the court in the Astroballe arena, you might have seen him on his way to a cryotherapy session or tirelessly repeating sequences of shots. His extended

"He's as skilled with a pencil as he is with a ball in his hand."

MATTHEW STRAZEL, TEAMMATE AT ASVEL AND THE U19 NATIONAL TEAM

absence had somewhat reduced the uninterrupted flow of articles and videos chronicling his every move. But in late January 2022, ESPN analysts still had the Nanterre-trained player from Le Chesnay (*département* of Yvelines) at the top of their predictions for the 2023 NBA Draft, which even at that time did not seem to surprise or worry him too much. "It doesn't shock me, doesn't unsettle me. I expect no less from myself. That's what I'm working for," he simply said.

In the light of a bay window overlooking the upscale district of Lyon where he has taken up residence, Wembanyama is curled up on his couch wearing a T-shirt signed with the Nike comma in vintage font. He looks proudly at the wall where his 90s painting hangs. "I fell in love with it immediately. It has a Spike Lee vibe, it's old school. It speaks to me. I like the posture, the drawing's balanced, all the space occupied, every centimeter calculated and precise."

Just like the words of the young man who officially became an adult on January 4— "I felt a bit sad to leave the world of childhood"—and whose passion for art nourishes his daily life.

Since he was at school, samurai and heroic fantasy characters have haunted the notebooks he fills with sketches. Reading the

Asterix books inspired him with ideas for characters who could join the world of Gaul. After training sessions at ASVEL, it was not uncommon for him to take over T.J. Parker's whiteboard in the locker room and fill it with marker pen drawings.

"He drew us a soccer player doing an acrobatic flip, and Karaba, the witch of Kirikou," (from the French animated adventure fantasy movie), laughs Matthew Strazel, his friend, former Villeurbanne teammate, and member of the U19 World Cup team, which lost in the final to the USA (81-83) in the summer of 2021. "He's as skilled with a pencil as he is with a ball in his hand. He does it without any kind of model. That's a reflection of his personality. He's a bit superstitious and is all about detail. Before I met him, I was intrigued by what people said about him. His humility shocked me. You'd think that all the hype around him might go to his head. In fact it's the opposite. He follows his path in silence, puts himself in his bubble, and works hard. It took him a bit of time to adapt when he arrived at Villeurbanne, but he's moving faster and faster and his progress will soon start to show."

A dedicated team, even more specialized and extensive than the one set up by Nanterre, whose financial resources are not on the scale of Tony Parker's club (budget of around $16m), works on the development of the player observers describe as a potential French Kareem Abdul-Jabbar. His profile is often compared to Kevin Durant or Giannis Antetokounmpo. Wembanyama says he analyzes the games of the two superstars in isolated camera view to gain inspiration. "But while also building my own game, my own philosophy," adds the Michael Jordan

fan, who is also fascinated by Kobe Bryant's work ethic.

Wembanyama's days are organized around his five daily meals, with nutritionist Julien Rebeyrol calculating his daily intake and then sending the order to a caterer who delivers the meals to his home. Fitting in around this are basketball sessions focused on individual development (Joseph Gomis and Pierric Poupet) and shooting, but also physical training (Manuel Lacroix, Julien Lenne), strength training and weightlifting, treatments, and even neuro-training sessions.

"He's been unlucky with injuries, but we've made sure he hasn't lost any unnecessary time," says Joseph Gomis. "We worked on his left hand, his finishing, footwork, explosiveness, stance, and approaches to the basket. Then when his shoulder blade was sufficiently recovered, we started working on his strong side again, with small loads. He's still young so you have to do things gradually and with meticulous care. He's very mature for his age. He always observes a situation before reacting to something or saying what he thinks. His basketball IQ has already developed significantly. But only match play will allow him to keep getting better. I'm also impressed by his ability to cut himself off from everything around him, from all the requests for his time."

Which continue to arrive from pretty much everywhere. The constant stream is managed by his parents, Félix and Élodie, together with Élodie's cousin, Nicolas de Fautereau, cofounder of marketing agency Willie Beamen—who has since ceded these duties to Issa Mboh, Wemby's media manager. "We channel requests via an email

"INDIVIDUAL AWARDS ARE GOOD, BUT I'LL NEVER BE SATISFIED IF MY TEAM LOSES."

Victor Wembanyama

address on his Instagram profile [93,600 followers in February 2022, more than 2.3 million after he was drafted in the summer of 2023, 3.5 million by the end of that year], to stop it from getting out of hand," explained De Fautereau. "If you say yes to everything, you get sucked into a never-ending spiral and can end up losing yourself. The important thing is to let him develop at his own pace."

His family, which shares similarities with the French Tillie siblings (a French family of basketball and volleyball players and coaches), is a guiding light for Victor. His younger brother Oscar switched from handball to basketball and joined the youth setup of Nanterre and then ASVEL. His older sister Ève was crowned U16 European champion in 2017 with Bourges and has played for Calais and Monaco (LF2). "When we get together, which is becoming increasingly rare, we never eat in front of the TV. We don't talk basketball.

We prefer to chat, joke around, and play board games—Gang of Four, Scrabble, and Codenames," says Wemby.

"They grew up in a sporting environment, but we never exerted any pressure or pushed our children to perform, or projected dreams onto them that weren't their own," adds his mother, who trained her son as a child. "We're a bit protective and vigilant with Victor. We don't want to overexpose him. But we realize it's inevitable, and the truth is he manages it very well on his own. We're so impressed with him and full of admiration. I wouldn't say it's a surprise, however … It goes with his personality. Even as a child, he was the son every parent dreams of. He slept through the night, was caring, kind, and loving. He did do a few goofy things too, and still does." [*Laughs*]

Victor's hobbies are not limited to drawing. Although he has a console connected to his flatscreen, it's not where he spends his evenings. His Instagram displays 10,000 message requests which he ignores, preferring to spend his free time reading—the fantasy epic *The Witcher* by Andrzej Sakowski, for example—or building LEGO. One of his latest acquisitions is the Star Wars Republic Gunship with 3,300 pieces. "Like all young people, I like video games and series. During lockdown in the Covid pandemic, we searched around in my parents' attic and found some old junk and treasures, including a Super Nintendo. There was also a Mario that didn't work [*laughs*], but we had a good time. But I honestly don't like being glued to the screen. I'm not addicted and I don't spend eight hours a day on it. In the evening before sleeping, I read. Although at the moment it's the highway code [rules of the road]." [*Laughs*]

Despite all this, basketball is never far away. Alongside the LEGO models on display in his living room, the trophies and medals he has already accumulated in his young career are displayed in Plexiglass cabinets. These include his prizes for best young player and most blocks in the 2021 French championship, and his silver medal from the U19 World Cup, which still stings even now. "Individual awards are good … But I've thought about that defeat every day since it happened on July 11. I'll never be satisfied if my team loses," he sighed, both frustrated and impatient to take his revenge at the earliest opportunity. ●

"WE NEVER EXERTED ANY PRESSURE OR PUSHED OUR CHILDREN TO PERFORM, OR PROJECTED DREAMS ONTO THEM THAT WEREN'T THEIR OWN."

Élodie de Fautereau, Wemby's mother

YOU HAVE TO SHOCK, ALWAYS SHOCK

ON NOVEMBER 11, 2022, AT 18 YEARS OLD, VICTOR WEMBANYAMA IS PREPARING TO PLAY HIS FIRST GAME FOR LES BLEUS IN LITHUANIA. THE DEBUT OF A PLAYER IN THE FRENCH NATIONAL TEAM HAS NEVER BEEN SURROUNDED BY SO MUCH HYPE. EXPECTATIONS THAT HE EMBRACES AND ACCEPTS WITH DISCONCERTING MATURITY AND EASE.

IN-DEPTH INTERVIEW PUBLISHED ON THE FRONT PAGE OF *L'ÉQUIPE*, NOVEMBER 11, 2022

KAUNAS (LITHUANIA)—A small group of around ten local journalists took up their positions in the arrivals hall of Kaunas airport on November 10, 2022; the welcome committee was to greet the arrival of the French team in Lithuania, and in particular one of their players. The cameras suddenly shot up to the ceiling to capture Victor walking by (officially measuring 7ft 2½ in at the end of that year). Headphones on his ears, he let out a smile and headed straight to the bus taking his team to Panevezys, where Vincent Collet's men are trying to qualify for the 2023 World Cup.

In a rejuvenated team full of new faces, the Boulogne-Levallois power forward, after a monumental start to the season marked as much by his performances in the French championship as the buzz caused in the USA by his visit to Las Vegas, will make the most anticipated debut of a French

player since Tony Parker. At 18 years old, he's already expected to play a major role in the team.

Against Lithuania, he will be subject to the same scrutiny he received during his recent press conference in Nanterre, where the media turned up in large numbers to try and unravel the mystery and personality of a player with unique attributes and limitless ambitions. During his Villeurbanne season, Wembanyama granted sports daily *L'Équipe* more than two hours of interviews. The words that follow are a combination of his public appearances in the run-up to the Lithuanian international competition, and his thoughts on that special afternoon in February 2022 when he gave us rare access to his inner world. On that occasion, we could already sense a young man with a maturity and wit striking for his age, and could see why the future—not only of basketball, but of all French sport—would inevitably revolve around him.

HIS DEBUT IN BLUE
"Fighting for your country gives you inner energy"

How do you see your debut in blue?
I've had this strong feeling about the national jersey since the youth teams. The motivation now is even stronger. Fighting for your country gives you extra inner energy. I'll try to adjust as best I can. In the international game, everything starts with defense. I hope I'll bring freshness and presence. I wouldn't say I hope to play or dominate straight away like with Boulogne. The first thing will be to adapt to the level. Then the aim is always to win, in any way we can. That comes ahead of my performance.

Does a particular moment in the history of the French team stand out for you?
I followed the Olympic Games in London

and Rio. But if there's one memory, it would be Nicolas Batum's block in the semifinal of the Tokyo Olympics [against Slovenia to qualify for the final]. The other thing that stands out for me is when I arrived in the pro league with Nanterre and ASVEL and started playing against or with players like Charles Kahudi and Antoine Diot who I watched as a kid.

How does the French team fit in with your plans? Do you plan to answer the call each summer?
Playing for the national team is only a few months of the year, but that doesn't make it any less important, and it will always be in the back of my mind.

"LOSING CAN MAKE ME A BIT CRAZY AND CAUSES INTENSE AGITATION THAT I CAN'T EXPRESS FREELY... BECAUSE I HAVE TO STAY CIVILIZED." [LAUGHS]

In the U19s, you played in a World Cup final in the summer of 2021 (lost against the USA 81-83, 22 points, 8 rebounds, 8 blocks). What do you remember about it?
I'd never been so stoked for a team or a competition. When everything suddenly collapses—out for five fouls before the end of the game—when you're in touching distance of your dream, it's hard. Just thinking about it makes my jaw tighten. It's a regret, an unchecked box inside me that I need to put right. Losing can make me a bit crazy and causes intense agitation, an instinct that I can't express freely because I have to stay civilized. [*Laughs*] I have a need to win. I've picked up lots of individual trophies in youth teams—most blocks of this, All-Star of that, and so on. That's good, but I can't feel fulfilled and proud if my team loses. Because, to put it simply, I don't like anyone to be better than me. Really don't like it at all. [*Smiles*]

Where does this "agitation" come from?
I think it's innate. Because my parents never pushed me to be absolutely the best. It was always my goal. They simply supported me.

HIS FAMILY AND CHILDHOOD
"If I'd wanted to be a lawyer..."

You were a goalkeeper in soccer and tried your hand at judo. Where does your passion for basketball come from?
As far back as I can remember, I always wanted to play in the NBA. It was in my U12 and U13 years at Nanterre that I realized that's what I wanted to achieve, and I was willing to work for it. My coach Karim Boubekri inspired me with work based on individual and technical development. I discovered what it was like to work on myself and to work hard.

Your younger brother Oscar (ASVEL) and older sister Ève (Monaco) also play basketball. What's your relationship like with them?
We're very close. When we get together, it makes for great meals—I occasionally cook. I'm not a disaster if I have instructions. [*Laughs*] But we never sit in front of the TV. When Ève won the U16 European Championship in 2017 with Bourges, we were all there. It was a great moment, our family's first major title.

> ## "MANY PARENTS TRY TO LIVE OUT THEIR PERSONAL DREAMS THROUGH THEIR KIDS. MINE NEVER PUT PRESSURE ON ME. THEY WOULDN'T BE DISAPPOINTED IF I TOLD THEM I'M QUITTING BASKETBALL TOMORROW."

I felt proud and a bit like I'd been set a challenge. I thought, I need to bring home some trophies too. [*Smiles*]

What role did your parents play?
Many parents try to live out their personal dreams through their kids. Although mine were into sport, they never put pressure on me. They protect me without being invasive. Unlike many players who don't have that kind of background, I'm fortunate to have landed in a balanced family, not one that blocks your development. If I'd wanted to be a lawyer, they would have encouraged me and wouldn't be disappointed if I told them I'm quitting basketball tomorrow. They're cautious, respectful, and ambitious. My mother was a coach. I was on her teams when I was little, but she didn't train me to develop as an athlete—she stayed in her role as a mother. My father was a triple jumper [record of 51ft], long jumper [record of 24ft 4in], and ran the 100 meters in 11 seconds. I did track with him. He supported me, corrected me, and taught me to run properly.

THE PLAYER HE DREAMS OF BECOMING
"Creating my own character"

Which player in history is the living embodiment of basketball for you?
No one can match the influence of Michael Jordan. I'm also a huge fan of Kobe Bryant, who I think of almost every day since his death [in a helicopter accident on January 26, 2020]. His passing shocked me. I know his stats and records, but most of all I admire his attitude, his work ethic, his philosophy of how he approached the game. I try to push my limits every day by following his example. When I'm suffering, when I have doubts, I often wonder what Kobe would have done. And I know he would have done more. So I go again.

Are there any players you take inspiration from?
I don't watch many games for entertainment. I observe to learn. I do that with Kevin Durant and Giannis Antetokounmpo [who he has often been compared to, and from whom he inherited one of his nicknames, "French Freak," in an echo of "Greek Freak"], their technique, their moves, their attitude. I try to steal a few things from them and apply them in games.

People often say you're a guard in the body of a center. They compare you to Ralph Sampson (the 7ft 4in "big" and number one in the 1983 Draft) or legend Kareem Abdul-Jabbar. What do you think about that?
To say I play as a guard would be to restrict my objectives and my repertoire. I'd like to play in all positions. It all depends on the opponent and who's defending against me. I want to be able to do everything, to evolve into a center or guard. That's what I'm trying to do when it comes to working on skills. At the end of the day, I just want to be myself and create my own character.

Like with the one-legged three after a crossover dribble that we saw you do with Boulogne against Limoges?

A BASKETBALL PLAYER LIKE A CHESS PLAYER

It was something I'd mastered after working on it for months. It's in my nature to continue to innovate. Scoring lots of points, getting more and more rebounds, putting up blocks is all well and good. But at some point, opponents adapt. You have to surprise them— shock, always shock. One day I'd like to become undefendable, a versatile player who can adapt to any situation, as much a defender as an attacker. A basketball player like a chess player, capable of anticipating every move my opponents make, and having the answer.

Are you saying you want to become the ultimate basketball player?
I know I'm only a young 18-year-old player and I need to stay as true to myself as possible. But I have ambitions, and more than confidence, I have faith in myself. What inspires me about the great players is the idea of creating my own philosophy, my own game, something new. And I have no doubt that if I choose the right path, with my unique roots, I'll be able to achieve my goals.

What are those goals?
Different things in the short, medium, and long term. I'll keep most of them to myself.

YOU HAVE TO SHOCK, ALWAYS SHOCK

When I knew that I wanted to play in the NBA, I quickly realized I also wanted to win a title. I can also share that I want to be number one in the Draft [this interview took place one year and four months before the event]. I don't expect anything less, because I know I've been really working for it.

MEDIA MADNESS
"I've been preparing for it since I was born"

Your games in Las Vegas with the Metropolitans in early October (36 and 37 points) against a team of prospects from the G League Ignite were watched by two hundred representatives from NBA franchises, creating unprecedented hype. *The New York Times* and *Sports Illustrated* came to Paris to follow you. How are you handling this media tidal wave?
Honestly, I'm finding it OK. There's a lot of attention, a lot of requests, but it's not new. I've been preparing for it since I was born. The more time goes on, the closer I feel to the challenges I've set myself. It increases my concentration and excitement. I've never felt so focused.

And when you hear LeBron James himself call you an "alien" or Stephen Curry compare you to a video game character, doesn't that affect you?
My life hasn't changed because of it. No words in the world can be more validating or go beyond the realization of the vision I have for myself. What it's mostly given me is more media work. [*Laughs*] But it didn't make me tense. I function best when I have lots to do. That's how I want to live my life.

"I'M A HUMAN BEING WHO WANTS SELF-FULFILLMENT FROM A PERSONAL AND PHILOSOPHICAL POINT OF VIEW. ON THE DAY OF MY DEATH, I DON'T WANT TO HAVE ANY REGRETS."

Do you feel any pressure from the expectations around you?
I try to be relaxed. I play basketball, I enjoy it, and I have fun. I'm all about the cool attitude. I don't like to get worked up about things. Because I'm fully aware of my ambitions and my determination, everything that's happening to me feels logical. And the demands I make of myself coincide with those expectations.

Thousands of articles are coming out about you and your game, most of them being written without having had the chance to meet you. Can you tell us in a nutshell who you are?
I'm a person, a human being who wants self-fulfillment and a successful life from a personal and philosophical point of view, in the sense that on the day of my death, I don't want to have any regrets. I want to have achieved everything I set out to achieve, and to be happy. There you go. You know me better than my mother now! Happy with that? [*Bursts out laughing*] ●

When Wemby met Yoda

A FAN OF *STAR WARS*, VICTOR WEMBANYAMA HAS FOUND THE PERFECT MENTOR IN INDIVIDUAL DEVELOPMENT COACH TIM MARTIN, ALSO KNOWN AS YODA BY HIS OTHER PADAWANS.

LEVALLOIS—His yell echoed around the empty corridors of the Marcel-Cerdan arena in Levallois. If Victor's roar of laughter was anything to go by, the words chosen by Tim Martin on that day in late January 2023 could not have been that serious. They did not stop the Metropolitans power forward from converting his free throw. Shouting in the middle of a drill, setting him a math test ("Vic, 92 x 2?"), reciting a philosophical quote or yelling a simple "honk!," asking his player what he had for breakfast, or even throwing himself on the court … Anything goes when it comes to distracting his disciple.

This is just one side of the technical Rubik's Cube developed by the 36-year-old US coach, a specialist in individual development and known by his Padawans in the NBA (Nic Claxton, P. J. Washington, Myles Turner, Tyrese Maxey) as Yoda. Martin gained Wembanyama's trust back in 2020, but not just because the new Spurs player is crazy about *Star Wars*.

"Yoda?," laughs the impeccably conditioned 30-something from Dallas. "It's touching that players trust me so much, but I don't see myself as a guru. I'm just someone who works hard and is convinced that we can learn something new every day," adds the man who mastered "the Force" during a tough childhood.

When we walked into the Marcel-Cerdan arena a little earlier, we saw Martin typing frantically on his laptop, while the player from Versailles was galloping around under the orders of Vincent Collet. During a break, he brandished his smartphone for a quick debrief with Wemby. "I take lots of notes.

WHEN WEMBY MET YODA

It's important for players to know what they are, to know what they can improve on—efficiency on layups, on a particular type of shot," says Martin. "After that, what interests me when I observe him isn't whether he misses a shot, but more how he set up to take it. If the shot's short, I set his feet, hips, posture, placement of hands on the ball, angle of his elbows. I'm looking for patterns, repeated mechanical errors, to make him aware of them and create habits so he can progress faster. Like an architect, we're building the foundations."

The relationship between the two men first began on Zoom, in the middle of the Covid pandemic. Their first contact was combined with an intense training session featuring footwork and a challenge: "100 three-pointers in ten minutes. I thought he was going to pass out," remembers the Jedi Master with a smile.

"I wanted to test him, push him without any kind of break. I learned the French word 'allez, allez, allez' that day. [*Laughs*] I would say he shot 70. Since then, he's made the 100." Their bond was solidified over mainly summer sessions, for example in Dallas, where the player spent three weeks in 2022 with Martin, who also has Rudy Gobert on his books and works in the training camps of the ComSport agency each summer.

The occasionally unorthodox methods of Martin appeal to Wembanyama. "Victor is on another level intellectually. He has a good attitude to life; I like his thought process. He's eccentric, like me, in a good way. I don't see the world like most people do. I look at the details, I love art. My maternal grandfather was a painter," says the man who plays Johann Sebastian Bach and Beethoven as much as Al Green or Aretha Franklin during his training sessions. "Being hot listening to aggressive hip-hop or Drake is easy. But can you also find your rhythm listening to classical music or softer vibes?"

He also draws inspiration from other disciplines to enhance his playbook. "I like boxing as it teaches players to be light on their feet. If you move like a boxer when you dribble, it's impossible for the defender to know where you're going next."

"People use the expression 'sky's the limit,' but that's not correct. There's no limit to what he can become. Beyond the sky, you have a whole universe to explore, right?"

TIM MARTIN

Born to an absent African-American father who worked in the music industry—he only found out in high school that he had been road manager for hip-hop legend 2Pac and the band NWA—and a Bohemian mother who had him at the age of 20, Martin could have had a radically different destiny. Placed in a children's home at birth, he was two years old when his mother took him back.

From then on, he grew up constantly on the move, attending 11 schools in 12 years. Living in an RV between Utah, New Mexico, Colorado, and Arizona in the land of Native Americans—the "Four Corners"—he had to adapt to many different environments, and this now informs his rich philosophy of life as a coach.

"I connected with so many cultures and religions, drinking it all in. At school, I was bullied because of being mixed race—not white enough for white people, and not black enough for black folks. I was looking for my place in the world. I was angry at my father for not being there—at least until my son was born." Basketball became a way out and then a visceral passion. "It was the only friend I kept with me wherever I went. I spent my life in gyms. I became obsessed with the orange ball. A mad scientist willing to try anything out on my students." [*Laughs*]

His bad luck continued into adulthood. When he separated from his son's mother in 2013, Martin found himself homeless at the age of 25. A passionate reader, he spent many afternoons sitting among the shelves of Barnes & Noble reading novels, personal development books (*Think and Grow Rich* by Napoleon Hill), and memoirs of famous coaches. He binged on FIBA coaching clinics on YouTube. Although he started his individual coaching business at the age of 15, and via people he knew, started working with Trae Young and Mavericks players Devin Harris and Josh Howard, he was not yet making a decent living, having to sleep in the back seat of his car, and shower and brush his teeth in the recreation center where he worked.

Then one day Martin met a banker called Glen Mastey. "He was the parent of a kid who played in an elementary school team I was coaching. He heard about my situation and wrote me a check for $600. At the time that was like a million for me. He took me to his office and taught me how to monetize my expertise. He helped me find an apartment and acted as a guarantor. It changed my life."

Today, Martin is now helping to change the life of Victor Wembanyama by tweaking his game here and there, and setting no ceiling for his Padawan. "People use the expression 'sky's the limit,' but that's not correct. There's no limit to what he can become. Beyond the sky, you have a whole universe to explore, right? Galaxies far, far away." [*Smiles*] A final assessment that George Lucas would not disagree with.

CHAPTER 13

ASVEL: THE ONE THAT GOT AWAY

VICTOR WEMBANYAMA AND VILLEURBANNE, A CLUB WITH 21 NATIONAL LEAGUE TITLES, SEEMED MADE FOR EACH OTHER. PRESIDENT TONY PARKER, THE BEST PLAYER IN THE HISTORY OF FRENCH BASKETBALL, MANAGED TO ENROL ITS GREATEST PROSPECT. BUT NOT HOLD ONTO HIM.

A story of the one that got away from ASVEL, the most successful club in the history of the French championship. It's the day before the first game of the 2022 final, which Villeurbanne would go on to win after an epic and thrilling finish against Monaco (3-2, 84-82 after overtime in the final game). Their performance is magnificent, historic, a feat not seen since the glory days of Limoges from 1988 to 1990. But it's overshadowed by bad news.

Tony Parker's organization is mid-preparation for the clash between the two Betclic Élite EuroLeague teams when it learns that Victor plans to quit the team, despite having another optional year left in his deal. The news is like a bombshell. Crowned champion without playing in the final due to injury, Wembanyama was only to spend one season in the *département* of Rhône, a season cut short by multiple injuries (high fever, broken finger, shoulder blade, psoas muscle).

In retrospect, his decision was a no-brainer. By returning to the Île-de-France with Metropolitans 92, Victor would no longer play in the EuroLeague and EuroCup. But he would be at the center of everything., exactly what he was looking for in his last season before the big move to the NBA. At ASVEL, he averaged 9.4 points and 5.1 rebounds in an average 18 minutes over 16 games, but on his arrival at Boulogne-Levallois, the Mets put him firmly in the driver's seat. He goes on to crush the 2022–2023 season and the league: MVP, top scorer (21.6 points), most rebounds (10.4 taken), blocks (3.2), best young player, and best defender. He has only just celebrated his 19th birthday in January 2023. In terms of media coverage, his fame spreads exponentially after two exhibition games in Las Vegas the previous October (36 and 37 points), before a mind-blowing debut with the French national team in November.

Each time he plays his former team, he seems to have even more motivation, as in Levallois when he scored the victory tip-in on January 9, 2023, (84-83), or in the last four, when he definitively eliminated the three-time defending champions to make his young Mets team and buddy Bilal Coulibaly delirious and unexpected finalists. As if sending a message.

How did ASVEL let the greatest ever talent in French basketball slip through its fingers when it had Tony Parker as president?

ASVEL, THE IMPOSSIBLE EQUATION

Neither party will admit to the slightest problem between them. Now connected through their affiliation with the San Antonio Spurs, TP and Wemby even appeared together all smiles in Parker's Texan residence at the beginning of July, as they watched the world finals of the French U19 team (beaten by Spain). Since his departure from ASVEL, Wembanyama has had only respectful things to say about a club that created a five-star setup to foster his development: two apartments, a dedicated team—physical and basketball trainers, medical staff, and dietician—to support him.

On June 18, 2022, Tony Parker declares to Lyon-based regional daily *Le Progrès* that he "absolutely wants to keep Victor" and is personally involved in the matter. All in vain. On the 26th, the day after ASVEL wins its 21st French championship crown, the divorce goes through. Why did he leave? And if he had stayed in the Rhône, would he have shone as much as he did with the Mets? The answer is in the question. A big budget setup with a five-star roster dominated by the grueling schedule of the EuroLeague, ASVEL could not have revolved solely around the star of Wembanyama. And it's difficult to see how a tour in Vegas could have worked with the approaching EuroLeague season. And in principle it would have stopped him from playing for the French national team too. "Being at the center of a group built for

"If Victor had smashed it with ASVEL, it would have suited everyone. But if we analyze the situation with the perspective we have now, in hindsight, it was simply impossible."

me is one of the things I came looking for," Wembanyama said at the LNB Media Day in late September 2022. "It was basically a collision between three projects with contradictory priorities," explains an informed observer of the situation. "That of Tony Parker and ASVEL [winning the EuroLeague], of a young coach, T.J. Parker, wanting to make his mark, and of an outstanding talent still under construction. If Victor had smashed it with ASVEL, it would have suited everyone. But if we analyze the situation with the perspective we have now, it was simply impossible." Others talk about rumors of misunderstandings, and questions around how T.J. Parker used him on the court, which would have created tensions with his representatives.

"Whenever he stayed in the rotation, he was great," says the coach. "But it was hard with his absences, because you put things in place, and reintegrating a player takes time … But there was never any problem between him and me. Did we miss something? We can always do better, but we did our best, and we can't be in his head making the decision for him. The plan was to develop him in the first year, and give him a major role in the second. I'm sorry he didn't have sufficient confidence in us to carry on. Because wherever he goes,

he'll be a success. And whatever happens, it's great for French basketball."

PARIS: HOPES DASHED

The file lies hidden at the bottom of a closet in an office in the Carpentier arena—out of sight to avoid retriggering the trauma. The document is from the agency ComSport and addressed to the club Paris Basketball. It contains a contract proposal and details of specifications to approve the signing of Wembanyama after his departure from ASVEL. The young organization founded by the American David Kahn in 2018 was originally going to be the next promised land for the prodigy, despite the interest of EuroLeague teams, his first pro club Nanterre. which tried in vain to bring him back, and the G League Ignite (NBA minor league), ready to offer him a seven-figure salary.

Informed of a potential deal in May, the Parisian club, which does not have the budget and infrastructure of ASVEL, struggles to meet the conditions, while remaining cautious about the outcome of a deal that is by nature explosive, competitive, and uncertain. But Paris has the profile: a young team with strong potential, led by a coach renowned for his training abilities, Jean-Christophe Prat. It also offers outstanding marketing expertise, and the French capital is an ideal setting for making Wembanyama the face of Parisian basketball before he takes off for the US. Two video conferences are organized between Prat and the player. In the end, they fail to prevent Wembanyama from switching to Levallois and the Mets, right at the buzzer. Under what conditions? "No comment" from Prat, and ditto from David Kahn. When contacted, the president of Paris Basketball, disappointed to have seen the diamond slip through his fingers, has always refused to discuss the matter.

BOULOGNE: COLLET, THE UNLIKELY U-TURN

It's all a bit blurry in terms of when the Metropolitans arrived on the scene. The very survival of the club was not even certain in the spring of 2022. The local council in Levallois threatened to kick them out of the Marcel-Cerdan arena, and Boulogne was considering withdrawing financially, its own arena project having hit the buffers. All this against a backdrop of rumored mergers

> **Being with Vincent was a critical factor. He's the greatest French coach—someone ambitious who respects my plans and the perfect person to lead me to the Draft.**

that never materialized with Paris and then Nanterre. When he heard about the possibility of recruiting Wembanyama, Vincent Collet, coach of the Mets and the French national team, nearly fell off his chair. And for good reason: he was planning to quit the Mets, his resignation letter already drafted by his lawyers.

"We didn't even think to enquire," he smiles. "It was the first day of training for the French national team [June 24, 2022]. I'd told the club I was leaving. I get a call from Bouna Ndiaye, who tells me he's had a meeting with Victor and his family, and apparently they wanted Victor to join me at the Mets. I spend an hour on the phone with the player. That was enough to convince me. It was a double opportunity: firstly, to work with the biggest prospect of all time in French basketball. And for the national team, it would also save a lot of time in terms of integrating him, as we already expected to see him play a prominent role in the team."

The final decision? Some think it was a clever power play orchestrated by his agents, whose stable includes Wembanyama, Collet, other Mets players (Jean-Paul Besson, Bilal Coulibaly), as well as two players drafted from Paris Basketball, Juhann Bégarin and Ismaël Kamagaté. Others view it as a choice linked to the environment, with a roster specifically built to orbit entirely around him, while also getting the full-time benefit of Collet's science. "Being with Vincent was a critical factor," the player said at the LNB Media Day. "He's the greatest French coach—someone ambitious who respects my plans and the perfect person to lead me to the Draft." What if it was as simple as that? ●

BEING 7FT 4IN TALL CONFERS UNDENIABLE ADVANTAGES...
AND DISADVANTAGES. PATRICK BASSET, VICTOR WEMBANYAMA'S
OSTEOPATH, WHO ALSO TREATED TONY PARKER THROUGHOUT
HIS CAREER, EXPLAINS MORE.

NEW HEIGHTS

"A billion." This is Victor's rough assessment of the number of times people have asked him what it's like to be so tall. At 7ft 4in on the height chart—or 10in higher than a standard door—this can be a huge bonus when you are a basketball player. But it can also pose many problems in terms of motor skills and coordination. As in many other areas of his life, the power forward of the San Antonio Spurs has managed to overcome these theoretical obstacles and turn them to his advantage. His osteopath, 71-year-old Patrick Basset, who treated Tony Parker throughout his career, has had Rudy Gobert and Evan Fournier on his table, and plans on regular travel to Texas to provide ongoing care for his new patient, explains further.

Patrick Basset: "Being tall inherently comes with positives and negatives. You have to make sure the advantages don't become disadvantages, and conversely, turn the drawbacks into strengths. Generally speaking, 'bigs' take longer to reach physical maturity, which is also reflected in their performance. This can have an impact in terms of motor, biomechanical, and psychomotor skills. For example, the arm is like a lever. The longer it is, the heavier the weight you're trying to lift and the more difficult the movement becomes. Big men also get small fractures more often, such as in the metatarsals and metacarpals.

"Movement in space can be a problem and has to be compensated for through highly developed three-dimensional vision. If growth spurts are too fast in people with tall frames this can have an impact in terms of precision, balance—linked to the higher center of gravity—instability in the muscular chains, as well as arm-leg and hand-eye coordination.

"But that's all in theory. Some will develop faster than others. Each case is unique. Victor is unique … With him, I apply a protocol I was already using with Tony [Parker] and have refined over 30 years. Like a system for scouting talent in soccer or basketball, it's a way of investigating and preventing self-injuries. It includes regular mechanical work with him, but also collaborative work with a whole team, including training, physical and mental conditioning, diet, biological data, and so on. I've been treating him for three years. When you take on a patient at 16 who you know hasn't finished growing, you have to adapt the work to facilitate that growth under the best conditions, so that the musculoskeletal system is in sync with each step. Because if you set up opposition between bone and tissue, you'll have a problem. Once an appraisal has been carried out, you can identify priority areas to focus on. It's about finding the right alchemy, like putting a puzzle together. All that work has resulted in a 2022–2023 season without injuries.

"You have to define standards based on body type and the objectives you want to reach—in this case sporting performance. In basketball, the slightest deficit will have an impact on play without the ball, receiving the ball, and speed of execution. In other words, elite athletes must know how to accept their size, understand it, and adapt it to what they want to achieve. Motor coordination between the arms and legs comes largely from the brain. In that sense, Victor is special, just as he is when it comes to basketball. The reactivity of his brain is exceptional. He's smart and proactive in terms of everything that happens to him on a physical level. It makes what he manages to do even more unique—his dribbling, super-low moves, one-legged shots—it doesn't look like the technique of a center!" •

"At ten years old, I was over 6ft 2in tall, towering over everyone's heads. But I've always tried not to feel like my size made me different from others. I wanted things to be on an equal footing. I was trying to play and improve as if I was short or average size. From a very young age, I've tried to do everything on the court. If you watch videos of me as a kid, you'll see I'm already going coast to coast and doing little layups."

" Turn the drawbacks into strengths "

Patrick Basset,
osteopath

CHAPTER 14

BLUE DREAM

FROM THE AZURE JERSEY OF METROPOLITANS 92 TO THE BLUE OF THE NATIONAL TEAM, WEMBANYAMA'S LAST YEAR AT THE BOULOGNE-LEVALLOIS CLUB WHERE HE COMPLETED HIS TRAINING WITH VINCENT COLLET, THE BEST COACH IN THE HISTORY OF FRENCH BASKETBALL AND HEAD COACH OF LES BLEUS, WAS THE IDEAL TRANSITION BEFORE THE BIG LEAP TO THE NBA.

The haunting whistled melody from the '90s iconic West Coast hip-hop track "Regulate" by Warren G fills the empty rows of the Marcel-Cerdan arena in Levallois. On the boards, the long frame of Victor Wembanyama contorts itself and weaves between Sacha Giffa, Steeve Ho You Fat, and Jean-Paul Besson. The object of the exercise: the art of cutting.

Vincent Collet, ball in hand, waits behind the three-point line for his player to get open and streak toward the basket so he can send the ball up into the clouds. Wembanyama takes off, hangs onto the rim with his left hand, then plunges his right arm into the hoop up to the elbow, in the style of Vince Carter in the 2000 NBA Slam Dunk Contest.

This is an example of how several times a week this season, the Boulogne-Levallois big man is treated to individual sessions with his trainer in addition to group work, weights, and other components of the plan created to prepare him for the big leap to the United States.

Wembanyama chose Boulogne-Levallois so that he could be as close as possible to the national team head coach, also known as "The Professor," and one of the finest hoops tacticians and trainers in the world. In return, Collet, who was about to leave the club, performed an immediate U-turn for the chance

to shape the greatest hope in the history of French basketball.

"He's on a clear trajectory to the stars," says the coach. "When I saw him for the first time aged 14 during an international window with the national team, it was a shock, a kid so tall and comfortable with the ball. The work we do together is like playing scales on the piano—the fundamentals, which can always be perfected, even if his are already solid. It's his inherent abilities that make him different. They're better than anyone I've coached before. That also creates and strengthens our relationship. We discuss his use, explore his game and learn from each other. I'm also discovering new things. It's not that common to work with a gifted person, because he is one, and not just on the court. You have to have a different approach. In terms of his

qualities, there are the obvious things like his measurements, motor skills, and so on. Then there are the plans he has for himself, his drive, and his self-reliance.

"You have to take all that into account—to give him freedom while also trying to influence his choices so that he continues to progress along the right path. He's a big fan of Kobe Bryant, and a bit like him, he's always wanting to learn, understand, and know why he's doing things. We try to make it make sense."

During the session, Collet takes the time to dissect and mime the movements and placements of the players in each position on the court so that Wembanyama can absorb them and understand the spaces where he can take advantage of his qualities and dominate.

"HE'S ON A CLEAR TRAJECTORY TO THE STARS. WHEN I SAW HIM FOR THE FIRST TIME AGED 14 DURING AN INTERNATIONAL WINDOW WITH THE NATIONAL TEAM, IT WAS A SHOCK."

VINCENT COLLET

The coach, who won the French championship with Le Mans (2006) and ASVEL (2009), explains between two drills: "You see, that's like a side-step in rugby," as he focuses on the subtleties of the pick and pop—his player's offensive and defensive options, how Argentinian Facundo Campazzo and Spaniard Sergio Rodriguez did it, their relationship with their big men, and so on. "Boris Diaw did it really well too," says the coach. "You have to master it, learn where to go and where not to go."

These sessions in the privacy of the sports arena, where the player from Le Chesnay learns about the finer points of the game he loves so much, are like rocket fuel for Wembanyama's development, nd one of the reasons why he decided to leave ASVEL and the EuroLeague. The top competition in Europe, its frenetic schedule would have limited the possibility of doing this type of individual work.

"He's just turned 19, an age where you make big leaps forward. It's astonishing, like with Bilal [Coulibaly]," says Collet. "In January to February [2023], he had seven or eight bad throws a game. And on the negative side, his shot selection wasn't good. He shot too much, too quickly from the three-point line. But when he's patient and works to get closer, he's almost undefendable, unstoppable.

The paradox is that even with difficult things, because of all the strings he has to his bow, he can do them. But he shouldn't just be assessed in terms of stunning moves like his one-legged three or his long-distance shot converted into a slam dunk … They impressed me too, but that's not what will determine who he becomes."

Like the hashtags accompanying his economical posts on social media, Victor is aiming to become "outtathisworld," a reference to LeBron James's description of him as an "alien" in October 2022 after his tour in Las Vegas. The background to the work carried out by Vincent Collet, and now Gregg Popovich in San Antonio, is in understanding a total player who has the unique ability, despite his natural role as a power forward, to play in any position and to have the answer to any problem posed by a defense.

"You can't define Victor in terms of interior play or the three-pointer," says the coach of Les Bleus. "His versatility is his strength. He has to learn to pull out the right trump card at the right time. I joked once that he could maybe play as a forward on the French team. But in reality, there's nothing to stop him doing so. Just because he's 7ft 4in tall, it doesn't mean he has to play near the hoop. His remarkable dribbling skills and super-high IQ are almost arguments for making him play point guard. In basketball, the point guard is the person who passes the ball most. In the modern game, this role often falls to position four. It would be presumptuous to claim we're creating the ultimate player with Victor. But I'm trying to help him grow so that he's armed for what awaits him next year [in the NBA] and … in future summers."

Because, of course, the destinies of Collet and Wembanyama are closely intertwined—both in terms of the mission that drove them this season with the Mets, who started from nothing and almost reached the top, and in terms of what awaits them in the French

"JUST BECAUSE HE'S 7FT 4IN TALL, IT DOESN'T MEAN HE HAS TO PLAY NEAR THE HOOP. HIS REMARKABLE DRIBBLING SKILLS AND SUPER-HIGH IQ ARE ALMOST ARGUMENTS FOR MAKING HIM PLAY POINT GUARD."

VINCENT COLLET

national team. The withdrawal of his future leader from the 2023 World Cup was a tough blow for the coach, but it changes little in terms of the real objective of this generation: the gold medal at the 2024 Paris Olympics. And at the center of the game, a Wembanyama who will have all the experience of an NBA season in his legs. The player has never attempted to hide his intentions. The French team is at the heart of his personal project. After the pain of losing the final of the 2021 U19 World Cup (81-83), he confidently dreams of "beating the USA in the final of the Olympics."

Boulogne-Levallois has therefore become not only a laboratory for his own progress, but also for the future of the national team. "Our connection is crucial," says Collet, "because as we've seen at the Mets this season [2022–2023], his destiny is to sooner or later become the leader of Les Bleus like Tony Parker was. I talk to him a lot about this leadership role—about becoming one

of those players who can pull out high-level performances, but also someone who can use that performance to make others better. His progress this season has been excellent, the best we could have hoped for. That will help the national team. Would his presence make us favorites at the Olympics? We were already contenders before him, and we were going to get given the label anyway." The task will now be to hold onto it for as long as possible. ●

"NEVER SEEN SUCH PERFECTIONISM"

"What has Vincent Collet given me? Everything that happened over the 2022–2023 season. Successful individual performances for me personally, and being part of a winning group, which is the most important thing for me. Also adaptation to opponents and consistency. What he does—I'd never seen that before in terms of analysis and technical and tactical perfectionism. He was the best person I could have spent my last year in France with. I've developed in terms of leadership and taking responsibility. In the history of the sport, I don't know if anyone has ever had as much responsibility in the championship as I did with the Mets. Vincent taught me and helped me learn how to bear that load."

Master mind

HIS EXCEPTIONAL HEIGHT IS NOT ENOUGH TO EXPLAIN THE TRAJECTORY OF COMET WEMBANYAMA, WHOSE BRAIN APPEARS TO WORK DIFFERENTLY AND FASTER THAN OTHERS.

"English? He learned it in his sleep!" Bouna Ndiaye roars with laughter. But Victor's agent is only half-joking. "I asked him how come he was so good at it. That's what he told me. What did he mean by that? That the senses and memory are working constantly, that he accumulated things during the day, and assimilated them at night."

When Wembanyama rolls out sentences in his precise English with a rounded American "r" and a barely perceptible French accent, it's difficult to believe that the young man has, until recently, never lived in the United States.

American journalists have pondered the same question, while being treated to his exquisite sense of a punchline: "If I was never born, I think Scoot Henderson would deserve the first spot," he said in Las Vegas during the Mets exhibition games in October 2022.

According to his inner circle, and going by the interviews we have conducted with him, Wemby is not only ahead on the court. He knows how to use his intelligence, which is as unusual as his measurements, to enhance his sporting performance. "Be original, do things differently" is a mantra for Wemby which he carries "in his soul," he says.

Bryan George, his U15 coach at Nanterre who now works as video coordinator with the Atlanta Hawks, remembers when his student changed the display language of his smartphone to English. "He told me that if he had to learn it, it was only right that he communicated in that language with the object he used most in his daily life. At age 13 …" recalls George, astounded.

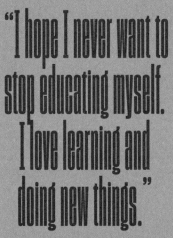

"I hope I never want to stop educating myself. I love learning and doing new things."

VICTOR WEMBANYAMA

The coach appointed Wembanyama as the "emotional leader" of his team, having seen his ability to create connections with his peers and bring them together. "He managed to reach everyone. In bad times, he gave out hugs. A problem with the referees? He was the first to slow things down. And if I was handed a technical foul, he was the one who came and calmed me down. [*Laughs*]

"He's uninhibited and sincere. And it's contagious. He needs that to flourish, it nourishes him. He sometimes offered to do the scoreboard on weekends. The kids do everything they can to avoid that! I told him: 'Do you have an incurable disease? Do you want to do a good deed so you can go to heaven?' [*Laughs*]

"He just thinks of others before himself. It's second nature to him," explains Ndiaye. "Like his open support and lobbying for his friend Bilal Coulibaly in the Draft. But he's been like that since he was little, to the point where it's shocking. I'd never seen that in a world where superstars always have an egocentric side."

His high school French teacher, François Salaün, recounted an eye-opening anecdote in an interview with Tania Ganguli of the *New York Times* in October 2022. When he asked his students to write an essay on achieving one of their dreams, the kids who loved basketball immediately wrote down the three critical letters in capitals: NBA. Not Wembanyama, who had written a short story called "Alice and Jules" with a friend.

It tells the story of a couple torn apart by an automobile accident caused by Jules

driving while drunk, who then fell into a coma and woke up having lost contact with Alice. Destiny would eventually bring the two soulmates together.

A relative claims that as a child, Wembanyama already knew how to read shortly after celebrating his third birthday. Not shy and gifted with a quickfire wit, he passed his baccalaureate with honors a year in advance, specializing in life sciences and economic and social sciences, despite already living at the grueling pace of a professional athlete for two seasons. "I hope I never want to stop educating myself. I love learning and doing new things," he said in September 2021.

"Even if he picks things up fast, it doesn't mean he's Einstein," laughs Frédéric Donnadieu, his first coach at Nanterre. "He's had his difficult moments in basketball. But you could feel his maturity even at ten years old. He was humble, polite, well brought up, and looked you in the eye when he spoke. You can talk to him about things outside basketball and have a really meaningful conversation. He's 'extra' ordinary in that sense."

"He's ahead in terms of everything—perspective, analysis," says Jérémy Medjana. "At 19, he's unique. He combines a competitive spirit with the ability to still be playful. For him, life is a game. Without that attitude, he'd be lost …"

Board game pro

Yes, games are everywhere. Whether with his teammates and coaches, or with his family at annual reunions, Wembanyama loves board games. "He likes to think, solve problems and equations," says Bryan George. "He's competitive and talented at it, quickly understanding how to tweak the rules and play around with them to make unexpected, magical moves. Just like he does in basketball."

His interests cover a spectrum as wide as his outstretched wingspan: LEGO, drawing, art, reading—especially heroic fantasy, which he voraciously devours—and in 2022 listed musical tastes ranging from Beethoven to Freeze Corleone and Alpha Wann as well as

Damso, Booba and 90s R&B. But even with such a level head and the caring and exceptional family environment he grew up in at Le Chesnay, Wembanyama could (should?) have buckled emotionally under the weight of the superlatives routinely applied to him, and the thousands of media requests asking for his time. On the contrary, at the age of 16, in front of a panel of 70 journalists at the 2021 LNB Media Day, he already demonstrated a disconcerting level of relaxation, a frank smile, and simple and clear answers, even allowing himself a joke or two with his audience.

Szechuan pepper and one-legged threes

"One day, we're at a restaurant. He's eating a dish and comes across something that makes him pull a face," recalls Ndiaye. "He asks me if I know about Szechuan pepper, tells me he just bit into a peppercorn, and launches into a five-minute presentation on why this Asian spice has a unique flavor. Sometimes he talks to me about the stars or semiprecious stones, like the bismuth he wore on his Draft suit. I can't keep up with his explanations. [*Laughs*] Let's not beat about the bush: he's a genius. He sees things we don't see. If you apply that type of intelligence to elite sport, it can't not have an impact … Lots of the things you see him achieving are driven by his own passion. The one-legged three? He worked on it for weeks, thinking no player of his size did it and that it would be unstoppable."

Wemby like Kobe

Vincent Collet, also known as "The Professor" because of all the young talents he has trained throughout his career, says much the same thing. The Mets and national team coach confirms the importance of intellect in learning. "He's exceptionally gifted, and not just with the ball in his hand. He already has many qualities, but intelligence is perhaps one of his greatest assets. It helps speed up the process, at an age when you're already progressing at breakneck speed. He was a fantastic leader despite the defeat. He's champion material," added the tactician after the defeat of the Mets in the championship final against Monaco, a team that his prodigy had no hesitation in placing among the 30 best in the world, NBA included.

In addition to his awareness of the trajectory he wants to take, Wembanyama has a winning mentality—"I hate losing, it causes intense agitation in me"—which his coaches and trainers detected very early on. "The way he raised his performance and concentration levels in high-pressure games in the U15 French championship left little room for doubt," explains Frédéric Donnadieu. Wembanyama draws inspiration from the memory of Kobe Bryant, for whom he has boundless admiration. "Since the day he died, I think about him almost every day. His work ethic, the 'Mamba Mentality,' it really motivates me to excel. I knew his stats and records. It was a shock when he left this world. When I think I can't go on, I wonder how far he would have gone. And I know he would have done more, would have gone further. So … I go again too," smiles Wemby. ●

JACKPOT IN VEGAS

INVITED BY THE NBA TO LAS VEGAS WITH METROPOLITANS 92 IN EARLY OCTOBER 2022, VICTOR WEMBANYAMA ACED THE TWO EXHIBITION GAMES ORGANIZED AGAINST THE G-LEAGUE IGNITE (37 AND 36 POINTS) AND IMPRESSED LEBRON JAMES AND STEPHEN CURRY. THIS WAS THE EPICENTER OF THE GLOBAL MEDIA EXPLOSION AROUND THE FRENCH PHENOMENON.

Already on the map of the NFL and the NHL, Las Vegas is still waiting for an NBA franchise. But from October 3–6, 2022, Sin City morphed into basketball central. It was the first adoptive home for Victor in the United States with an invitation to play two exhibition games with his Boulogne-Levallois club against the young players of Ignite, an outfit specialized in developing young talents in the G-League, the NBA's satellite development league.

It was a visit so successful that according to ESPN, the boss of the North American Championship, Adam Silver, promised "we will be watching 'tanking' closely in 2023." In other words, the strategy—condemned by the league—of losing as many games as possible and therefore creating more chance of getting first pick in the Draft, the only position from which it would be possible to select Wembanyama. The commissioner apparently read a report in the US media of a manager shouting "tank!" while laughing with colleagues after one of the young French player's games, because in two meetings the player from Le Chesnay shot 73 buckets. as well as the points, he also pulled moves out of the bag that have had scouts salivating for years, such as his three-pointers off the dribble or shot on one leg, both of which are unprecedented for a 7ft 4in player.

The word unprecedented could also be used to describe the Metropolitans 92 trip to Nevada. The idea of the NBA was hatched just after Wembanyama signed up in early July. "His agent Bouna Ndiaye suggested the trip to us. Twenty-four hours later, Shareef Abdur-Rahim [former NBA All-Star and president of the G-League] confirmed the invitation," explained Alain Weisz, director of sports operations for the Île-de-France club.

The French National Basketball League gave its blessing to the overseas excursion, slap-bang in the middle of the championship season, and a delegation of 24 people invaded the MGM Grand, one of the most famous hotels and casinos in Sin City, all expenses paid by the NBA.

At the top of the bill, a super-motivated star player. "It's something that's never been done before, and even less so for French basketball. A key part of my makeup is to innovate and create things that have never been seen before. I'm approaching this as the leading role. I want to do great things, especially at this event," said Wembanyama in a preamble to the 2022–2023 season.

On the court, the former Villeurbanne player put on an impressive show, cementing his spot at the top of the 2023 Draft. The NBA had pitted him against Scoot Henderson, the G-League Ignite guard, and Wembanyama's only potential rival in terms of who might get the first call onto the Barclays Center stage in Brooklyn on June 22,

2023. "Scoot Henderson? He's a really great player. If I was never born, I think he would deserve the first spot in the Draft," said the French big man to laughing journalists.

Twenty-four hours later, with 37 points and 5 blocks, Wembanyama buried the debate despite the defeat of Metropolitans 92 (115-122). The mentality of the prodigy trained at Nanterre also amazed those watching. His 28 points in the second half almost led the Île-de-France club to a cool holdup. "At times he was extraordinary," said his coach Vincent Collet.

In the revenge game two days later, the advantage went to Boulogne-Levallois (112-106) and the big man continued his show (36 points, 4 blocks) while Henderson had to leave the court after an injury to his right knee. Beyond the two matches themselves, the charm operation exceeded expectations. Seventy-five accredited journalists and around two hundred executives and staff from NBA franchises invaded a room with a usually hushed atmosphere. They all got to see Wembanyama's effortless ease in front of

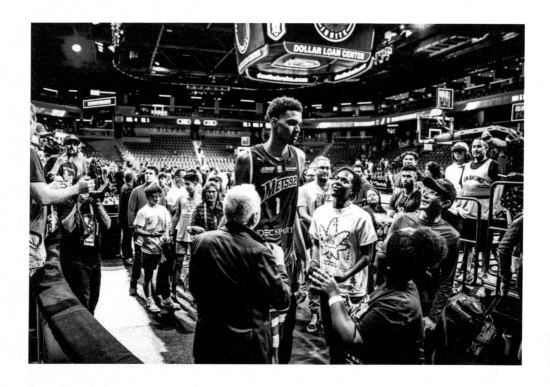

a microphone and his impeccable English. "I saw Yao Ming work out in Chicago in 2002. With no disrespect to the other international prospects who have emerged since then, including Luka Dončić, we haven't seen this kind of hype for an overseas player since Ming. How could you miss it?" summed up Marc Spears (ESPN).

Taking place in the middle of the uneventful NBA preseason, Wembanyama's two outings provided topics of conversation at the press conferences of stars from the big league. They were all asked for their thoughts on the French big man, both as a phenomenon and as a future opponent in the jersey of the San Antonio Spurs.

"Everybody's been a unicorn over the last few years, but he's more like an alien. No one has ever seen anyone like that," said Los Angeles Lakers small forward LeBron James, four-time champion and the NBA's all-time top scorer. Stephen Curry, winner of four rings and architect of the game's revolution to three-pointers, continued the chorus of praise. "He's like the 2K create-a-player [the NBA video game], every point guard that wants to be 7-foot. Cheat-code type vibes but he's a solid talent. It's great to watch," said the Golden State point guard.

Kevin Durant, NBA Finals MVP in 2017 and 2018, and Giannis Antetokounmpo, winner of the 2021 NBA championship with Milwaukee, were already anticipating their duels with Wembanyama. "We got to get ready for this kid. He's going to be really good," said the Greek-Nigerian big man. "The league's really in trouble when he comes in," added KD. "We got a 7-5 dude being able to do everything on the court. He's inspiring to a lot of people out here."

The dictates of the French championship season meant the NBA had to "return" Wembanyama to France on October 7, 2022, but already with a sense of loss. To compensate, a few weeks later the NBA signed an agreement with the French National Basketball League (LNB) to broadcast every Mets game on its platform, making the popularity rating

We don't have figures on the number of interview requests, simply because we lost count. We thought it would eventually die down, but it's gone up exponentially. It's a hurricane. "

ISSA MBOH, media manager

of the man it already sees as the icon of its future climb even higher.

The Big Bang in Vegas had multiple repercussions, particularly in terms of media coverage, in the months that followed. The *New York Times* traveled to the French capital; ESPN sent seven people to Paris for a documentary and to provide content to a section of its platform entirely dedicated to Wembanyama; *Sports Illustrated* and *Slam Magazine* displayed Wemby on the front page; while NBC attended the championship final at Roland-Garros. "We don't have figures on the number of interview requests, simply because we lost count," says Issa Mboh, responsible for centralizing press requests throughout the season preceding the Draft.

A phenomenon that he describes as "exponential" and "a hurricane," it left many French and international media outlets disappointed at requests that could not be met. In June 2023, in the madness of the Draft in New York, he concluded: "We thought it would die down after a while. But it's never stopped going up. As if there were no limits—just like Victor." ●

CHAPTER 16

One photo, one destiny

DUG OUT BY MICHAËL ALARD, ONE OF VICTOR WEMBANYAMA'S FIRST COACHES, A PROPHETIC SNAPSHOT WENT VIRAL ON THE NIGHT OF THE NBA DRAFT LOTTERY ON MAY 16, 2023, NEATLY ENCAPSULATING THE HISTORY, PATH, AND DESTINY OF THE UNICORN PLAYER.

The picture has a yellowish tint, not from the passing of time but from the pallid light of the Paul-Vaillant-Couturier sports complex in Nanterre and a hastily taken shot with a smartphone. In the gym where the club's youngsters train, as yet unrenovated in this 2014–2015 season, Victor Wembanyama, slightly blurred in the image, and his U11 coach Michaël Alard, wearing a "Nanterre Basketball" hoodie, pose for the camera. The beanpole of a boy has just joined the Hauts-de-Seine team, crowned surprise senior French champions in 2013, and is in his first season with the club. Wemby appears to have a faint smile on his lips. In his half-closed yet shining eyes, a mixture of innocence, confidence, and ambition can already be seen. Even more remarkable, he sports a San Antonio jersey emblazoned with Tony Parker's number nine. And so with one

click of a cell phone, the history, path, and destiny of the prodigy from Le Chesnay—and with him that of French basketball—were fixed forever in time in an unexpected, defining, and prophetic moment.

On May 16, 2023, the prediction of the oracle is within touching distance. It's the big night of the lottery to determine who will get first pick in the future NBA Draft, in other words, the team which, without a shadow of a doubt, will select Victor. It's a historic moment, celebrated with great fanfare by the Swoosh brand—the young star's shoe and apparel supplier—in its Parisian premises on the Champs-Élysées, in the presence of the player's family and French soccer star Kylian Mbappé. In an atmosphere of general euphoria, San Antonio comes out of the hat …

"The universe told me," exclaims Victor excitedly to ESPN. He would later explain

"The photo is a perfect representation of both his younger years and his future. Almost like it was written in the stars..."

MICHAËL ALARD

that he had filmed a video before the lottery where he expressed his conviction on camera that the Texans were going to hit the jackpot. Dug out by Michaël Alard on the celebratory evening and posted the next day, the photo of Wemby in the jersey with the spur immediately went viral. A case of prophecy? The 36-year-old coach is quick to debunk the appealing theory. "When a young talent joined the club, I got into the habit of taking a picture of them with me, but I only did it to compare their height to mine or to track their development. It was just for his height. [*Laughs*] It wasn't done for any special reason. It was interesting for Victor because I'm 6ft 4in. He was officially in the U11s but played in the U13s and was already almost the same height as me! And there's no particular anecdote related to the jersey. Was he in love with the Spurs? Did he talk about them all the time? Honestly, I can't remember and I don't think so. The truth is that when you stepped onto a basketball court or into an academy at the time, everyone had the TP jersey as he'd just been crowned NBA champion in 2014. It's a generational thing, like with Kylian Mbappé. Today, all the kids shoot three-pointers and wear Stephen Curry jerseys." As the draw continued, Alard watched the list of franchises unable to claim the first prize. The San Antonio scenario was shaping up nicely and the memory of the photo with his protégé suddenly popped into his head. He started frantically searching through his phone and eventually found the image. When he

posted it the next day, the buzz was immediate and global. The snapshot was reposted by the media, fans, and finally Wemby himself on his Instagram account.

"I thought it was cool to share it, but I didn't expect such a massive reaction," explains Alard. "I'm even almost embarrassed that it took on such proportions, especially for his parents to see an image of their then 11-year-old son suddenly going viral on social media without being able to give their agreement to it. What I find incredible is the combination of circumstances. I wouldn't have posted the photo if Victor hadn't been wearing a Spurs jersey and I hadn't been in a Nanterre hoodie. You can immediately recognize his still thin face, you can identify the place where he learned his craft, with one of his coaches. Many of us have followed and trained him but it's a nice nod for our club, as well as the one where he'll make his life's dream come true. It feels like a fairy tale. He landed at the Spurs? Surprise, surprise … The team is similar to him—smart, does things differently. That will suit Victor, who's a quick thinker and has an artistic side. The photo is a perfect representation of both his younger years and his future. Almost like it was written in the stars …" ●

★ WHAT WEMBY SAYS ★

"The universe told me"

"There's a special relation between France and the Spurs because of Tony Parker of course and also Boris Diaw [four titles for 'T.P.', and one for 'Babac' with his best friend in 2014]. I know half of the country, if not the whole country, wanted the Spurs to have the first pick. I was looking at everyone and everyone was happy, so I was too. The universe told me … Not to brag about it, but I knew what was going to happen. And I actually recorded myself saying it this morning walking to practice. So yeah. The universe told me. Dreams, feelings. It happens sometimes. But it's never wrong, it's always right." (to ESPN, May 16, 2023)

THE ALIEN IN NUMBERS

HIS SHOE SIZE

#1

Picked first in the Draft on Thursday, June 22, 2023, Victor Wembanyama became the highest drafted French player in history, while his teammate Bilal Coulibaly (picked 7th by Indiana and traded to Washington) equaled the previous record set by Killian Hayes.

#20.5

#7'4"

Or 2.24m. His official barefoot height. Only seven players in NBA history have been as tall or taller: Mark Eaton, Rik Smits, Shawn Bradley, Manute Bol, Yao Ming, Ralph Sampson, and Boban Marjanović. Between them, they posted a total of 78 three-pointers in their careers, regular season and Playoffs combined. In three pro seasons, Victor Wembanyama converted a hundred of them with Nanterre, ASVEL, and Boulogne-Levallois.

#15

Wemby took his first pro steps in the EuroCup on October 29, 2019, (65-73 loss to Brescia) at the age of 15 years, 9 months, and 25 days. Three days earlier, he appeared on a Betclic Élite roster sheet for the first time but stayed on the bench. He first played in the EuroLeague aged 17.

#8'

Or 2.43m. His wingspan, currently the largest for an NBA player, ahead of the 7ft 8in of Boban Marjanović and Mo Bamba. The absolute record belongs to Manute Bol (8ft 6in).

#100%

Wembanyama swept the board for all individual trophies: MVP (youngest player in history at 19 years, 4 months, and 14 days, ahead of Antoine Rigaudeau), best young player, best defender, top scorer, and the Thierry Rupert trophy for most blocks. An unprecedented grand slam in the history of the French National Basketball League.

He became the third player to score at least 500 points in the French championship before turning 19, after Antoine Rigaudeau and Tony Parker. He even broke through the 1,000 regular-season career points barrier.

#500

#21.6

His points average in the French championship (record of 33 points), unheard of since Rick Hughes in 2004 (SIG, 24.1), and Yann Bonato in 1995 (Paris BR, 23.3). Wemby finished top scorer but also had most rebounds (10.4), blocks (3.2), and the highest efficiency rating (26, not seen since 1996 and Paul Fortier on 27.1 with Le Mans).

BUSINESS

#350

In millions, the number of views generated by content mentioning or representing Victor Wembanyama in 2022–2023. This makes him the 8th most-engaging player on the social media platforms of the NBA, which broadcast Mets games from the end of October 2022. The ranking is dominated by LeBron James (1.3 billion) and Stephen Curry (881 million), but Wembanyama is ahead of Nikola Jokić (10th, 253 million), champion and MVP in the 2023 NBA final.

#3.3

In millions, the number of his Instagram followers at the beginning of 2024, already way ahead of all other French players in the NBA.

INTERNATIONAL

#20

Total points scored in his first game for the French national team, an easy victory in Lithuania (90-65) on November 11, 2022, where he even sat out the last quarter.

In the U19 World Cup in the summer of 2021, lost by France to the USA in the final (81-83), Victor Wembanyama, in the starting five of the competition, finished with 40 blocks in 7 games, an average of 5.7 blocks per game. A historic record, all categories combined, in a single FIBA tournament since this statistic was recorded.

#5.7

"ALIEN," "CHEAT-CODE"... WHAT THE STARS SAY ABOUT WEMBY

"Everybody's been a unicorn over the last few years, but he [Wembanyama] is more like an alien. No one has ever seen anyone as tall as he is but as fluid and as graceful as he is out on the floor. He's, for sure, a generational talent."

LEBRON JAMES (LA LAKERS)
Four-time champion and NBA all-time top scorer

"He's like the 2K create-a-player, every point guard that wants to be 7-foot. Cheat-code type vibes but he's a solid talent. It's great to watch."

STEPHEN CURRY (GOLDEN STATE)
Four titles with the Warriors

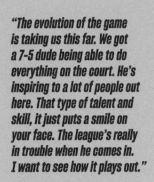

"The evolution of the game is taking us this far. We got a 7-5 dude being able to do everything on the court. He's inspiring to a lot of people out here. That type of talent and skill, it just puts a smile on your face. The league's really in trouble when he comes in. I want to see how it plays out."

KEVIN DURANT (PHOENIX)
Double NBA champion with Golden State

"He's not LeBron, Tim [Duncan], Kobe [Bryant], or anyone else. He's Victor and that's who we want him to be. Am I excited to coach him? I'd do a somersault, but I'd be out for three months." [Laughs]

GREGG POPOVICH (SAN ANTONIO)
Head coach of the Spurs, signed with the Texan franchise until 2028

"I believe in 2045 everybody's gonna look like Victor. His skills, the way he can shoot the ball, the way he can move, he's extremely fast for his size. He's unbelievable. He has the chance to be one of the best to ever play this game. We've never seen something like that before and I think it's a good challenge for everybody."

GIANNIS ANTETOKOUNMPO (MILWAUKEE)
2021 champion with the Bucks

CHAPTER 17

A NEW SHERIFF IN TOWN

VICTOR WEMBANYAMA HAS TAKEN TO HIS NEW TEXAN ENVIRONMENT LIKE A FISH TO WATER. AND DESPITE THE UPS AND DOWNS OF A DIFFICULT FIRST SPORTING SEASON, THE TRAJECTORY OF THE FRENCH COMET IS STILL FIRMLY ON TRACK.

Sporting a black cowboy hat, he stares inscrutably into the camera, breakfast taco in hand, against the backdrop of one of the countless murals depicting him in San Antonio. Victor seems right at home here. After just a few months, the young man from Le Chesnay has embraced the personality cult surrounding him in San Antonio, and the unique destiny promised to him in the seventh largest city of the United States. "They treat me like a member of their family. I'm very grateful to them," he says.

After renting a house near the downtown district, he has moved to a home of his own around 12 miles north of the city, in an oasis of greenery previously resided in by club legend David Robinson. The aim of the move is to be closer to the Victory Capital Performance Center, a brand-new training complex considered one of the most advanced in the world. "PSG has nothing to match it," those in the know tell us. It will now be the laboratory for his development.

He still has favorite hangouts in the city, like the French brasserie Mon Chou Chou in the upscale Pearl district, where he regularly orders the raclette cheese and Bayonne ham baguette or the roasted bone marrow, a server there tells Maxime Aubin from *L'Équipe*.

As a prelude to his season, Wemby played the tourist, visiting the must-see Fort Alamo, as well as touring the city's bars to get up close and personal with the fans. We also caught up with him at the end of January 2024 in the presence of Mayor Ron Nirenberg to celebrate the official accreditation of a French bilingual program in an international school. "The Spurs are a fundamental part of the city's culture," recalls Nirenberg. "Victor has brought back hope. He inspires others. He's created a new sense of unity in the city."

And on the court? After a dream start (3 wins-2 losses), reality caught up with a team undergoing a complete rebuild. But that doesn't stop the franchise with five NBA titles from forging ahead and, based on the flashes of genius exhibited by its new talisman, the early signs of a new golden age may be starting to emerge.

FIRST GAME

The atmosphere could be an NBA finals game. Victor Wembanyama's first press conference on October 2 generated a thousand requests for accreditations., as did the inaugural game against Dallas and Luka Dončić. This followed a successful pre-season featuring some galactic highlights—the dunk with outstretched arm reminiscent of Michael Jordan in the final scene of *Space Jam*—all brought to earth by the man LeBron James nicknamed "the alien." "I'm not shaking, but I have butterflies in my stomach," says the young player. He makes his entrance in a feverish Frost Bank Center packed to the rafters (18,947 fans).

The party won't be perfect. Restricted by foul trouble, despite the defeat (119-126), Wemby delivers a promising line of stats (15 points, 6-for-9, 5 rebounds) similar to those of Tim Duncan 26 years earlier (15 points, 10 rebounds). The Spurs would take their first victory two days later in another Texan derby against Houston (126-122 OT) with their French player scoring 21 points and 12 rebounds.

FIRST BIG SUCCESS

Dropping over 35 points in one of your first five games on the NBA stage? Only Shaquille O'Neal and Michael Jordan have done it faster than Wembanyama, managing it on their third attempt. It took Wemby five games to reach this first milestone: 38 points (at 15-for-26 and 10 rebounds). And he did it away from home, taking decisive action in the money time, in front of one of the candidates for the top of the Western Conference—Phoenix Suns' Kevin Durant, Devin Booker, and Bradley Beal. "It just makes me want to go even higher to beat all these records," says

Wemby. This is a precious moment in their season: the only time the Spurs will post a positive record (3-2), after winning twice in a row in Arizona. The hopes of a metamorphosis and a team capable of contesting the Playoffs are still alive as the Spurs finish firmly in last place in 2023 (15th with 22 wins).

FIRST DOWNER

After their excellent trip away, the Texan franchise experiences a spectacular fall from grace. While a third consecutive win is on the cards against Toronto, it slips out of reach (loss of 116-123 OT), marking the start of an inexorable descent. Eighteen defeats in a row, the worst losing streak in its history. We are suddenly reminded of how young the team is (the youngest in the league at an average age of 23.5), and its lack of experience. We also witness the bizarre and failed Jeremy Sochan experiment, where a power forward by training plays in the position of point guard, and the interior combo of Zach Collins-Victor Wembanyama, which pushes the French player out of the paint, his natural zone of domination, and encourages him to shoot more than is sensible from behind the arc. "Most defeats I've had? It was probably when I was playing soccer. We didn't have a good team," Wemby would joke to the local media, while also admitting his difficulty in engaging in an exercise he wasn't accustomed to: learning to lose and to be patient. San Antonio finally ends the losing streak on December 16 in the first duel between Wembanyama and LeBron James, with a victory over the LA Lakers (129-115) thanks to 36 points from Devin Vassell, and 13 points, 15 rebounds, and 2 blocks for the French player.

FIRST METAMORPHOSIS

The trailing foot of a ball boy in Dallas indirectly changes the course of Victor Wembanyama's season. Falling awkwardly on him during warmups for a game that he would not play, Wemby is forced to restrict his playing time, firstly by 25 minutes, and then by 30. He is also not allowed to compete in back-to-back games. Returned to the position of center during this period, the former protégé of Vincent Collet at Boulogne-Levallois and the Donnadieu brothers at Nanterre makes a huge leap forward. His productivity explodes. Over 10 matches, he scores at an incredible rate of nearly a point a minute—232 in 242 minutes, according to *The Athletic*—while making 62.5% of his 2-pointers, and also upping his defensive capabilities (5.2 blocks per game over a playing time extrapolated to 36 minutes). The visual evidence is impressive, featuring no shortage of surreal moves. Receiving better service from his team, especially point guard Tre Jones recently promoted to the rotation, Wemby regularly flies through the air to make the alley-oop.

In transition, he passes the ball behind his back before finishing with a dunk. On December 28 in Portland (118-105), he totals

"I'm not shaking but I have butterflies in my stomach."

VICTOR WEMBANYAMA

30 points (9-for-14), 6 rebounds, 6 assists, and 7 blocks in just 24 minutes. Facing the same Blazers a month later (116-100), he gets so high on a block that his hand wraps all the way around a shot by Anfernee Simons who can only watch in disbelief. "He's a freak of nature," Jeremy Sochan affectionately says about his teammate who gradually refines his passing precision with a growing taste for blind assists.

On January 11 in Detroit (130-108), he posts his first triple-double (16 points, 12 rebounds, 10 assists, all without a turnover), in just 21 minutes. Since the NBA started keeping records in the 1950s, only Russell Westbrook made these numbers more quickly in a game (20 minutes).
"I ain't no Spurs fan, you know this. But I watch them because of big fella," says Kevin Garnett on his podcast in conversation with

Already opponents in the final of the 2021 U19 World Cup, Wembanyama and Chet Holmgren (no. 7), who are also competing for the Rookie of the Year Award, represent the future of the NBA. On February 13 in Toronto, the French player, shown here imperiously blocking the Oklahoma City big man, achieved the first rookie triple-double with 10 blocks since David Robinson in 1990.

former teammate Paul Pierce in January 2024. "And big fella brings the show every night. When you come in and you start doing stuff that the whole NBA fraternity ain't seen, that's when you start putting your print on the league."

Facing Rudy Gobert's Minnesota on January 26, the Spurs' key game of the season (113-112), he wins the duel against his future teammate in the French national setup, cooking the former Cholet player with a "Shammgod," the lasso dribble popularized by Dejan Bodiroga. "The play's better quality. It also shows in the advanced stats, not just in the win-loss record," says Wemby about the Spurs who posted five wins in fourteen games in January. "For me personally, we've also managed to target my strengths and what I need to improve on. We've refined my game."

A FIRST ALL-STAR?

Without his team's results (10-40 on February 7 and bottom of the Western Conference), the impressive statistical performance of Victor Wembanyama would undoubtedly have taken him to the All-Star Game in his first season.

"What he's doing in a challenging situation, with restricted playing time, is just crazy," says French international Nicolas Batum. "In 36 minutes, he'd have the stats of an All-Star…" Over this length of playing time, the Basketball Reference website gives him 26 points, 13 rebounds, and 4 blocks, averages higher than those of David Robinson and Tim Duncan, previous number one Draft picks for the Spurs, in their first year, both of whom were officially recognized with a first star in the All-Star Game and the Rookie of the Year Award—a distinction Wembanyama is favorite for ahead of Chet Holmgren (Oklahoma City). The difference here is that at that time San Antonio were posting 56-win seasons. "I'm not worried about him," smiles the captain of the French team. "If he's not an All-Star this year, it will probably be the only time in his career!" ●

HIS MID-SEASON STATS

20.4 points (46.2% for field goals, 30.1% for 3-pointers), 10.3 rebounds, 3.2 assists, 3.1 blocks, 3.4 turnovers in 29 minutes

#THE BILLION

In 2023, the year he was drafted and made his international debut in the North American league, Victor Wembanyama generated 1.3 billion views or engagements on social media, surpassed only by the icons Stephen Curry (1.6 billion) and LeBron James (2.8 billion), the all-time leading scorer in NBA history ahead of Kareem Abdul-Jabbar. According to specialist forecasts, Wemby could also become the first NBA player to generate more than a billion dollars through his sporting agreements alone. His first contract is for $55 million over four years—the maximum authorized for a player drafted number one pick in 2023.

#3.1

Wemby's average number of blocks per game at the mid-season point. If he keeps up this pace, he will be the third rookie San Antonio Spurs player to dominate the league in blocks, after, of course, David Robinson and Tim Duncan.

#38

By scoring 38 points in his fifth game in Phoenix (132-121), the player from Le Chesnay has already achieved the fourth-best performance by a French player in the NBA (Tony Parker, 55 in 2008; Evan Fournier, 41 in 2022; Rodrigue Beaubois, 40 in 2010). He is also ranked fourth in jersey sales behind Stephen Curry, Jayson Tatum, and LeBron James, but ahead of Giannis Antetokounmpo and Luka Dončić.

"A TEMPERAMENT LIKE TIM DUNCAN"

WITH 28 SEASONS AND FIVE TITLES UNDER HIS BELT AS HEAD COACH OF THE SPURS, GREGG POPOVICH DESCRIBES VICTOR WEMBANYAMA'S QUALITIES AND THE PROMISES HE HOLDS FOR THE FUTURE.

"Being able to develop young people like Victor Wembanyama, making sure they start out on the right track, is the most rewarding part of my job. Everyone knows he's talented. But it's not just about talent. Michael Jordan's first title came in his seventh year. Nikola Jokić just won his first ring, and it took him eight years. We have every right to hope that things will go faster for Victor, but you can't skip steps. What's exciting about Victor is that he's got a temperament and character like Tim Duncan. You can easily coach him, whereas young people often think they know everything. He's confident in his abilities, but he's willing to learn and listen and knows how to deal with the positive and the negative.

"He plays center at times, and a lot of people see him that way because he's the tallest guy on the floor, but these days, there's no such thing as an old-fashioned point guard or center. Everything is interchangeable. So you can see Victor isolated on a wing, on the block, involved in a central pick and roll. Sometimes, he'll be the one holding the ball on this option or bringing it up after a rebound. He does everything, which is precisely what I expect of him. He also wants to and has the skill for it. We needed 20 or 30 games to see where he felt most at ease and what were the obvious things to correct. He had to adapt to the roughness of the game because he's got a target on his back, and everyone wants to get in his face physically. He tended to dribble too much in traffic because he's a good ball handler. He turns the ball over sometimes because of this, but so does everyone else. He quickly realized that he needed to dribble less to counter the speed and physical impact of his opponents. We try to establish strategies where he gets closer to the circle. His career is in its early stages, so we're working on his three-point shooting, balance, and consistency, knowing that all this will take time.

"We could have taken on a veteran to win more games straight away. But we didn't for two reasons. Firstly to keep our powder dry, in other words, waiting before spending for spending's sake, and retaining that financial room for maneuver. Once the structure is established, it will be important to add a few free agents. But it wouldn't have brought us a title immediately, and would have been wasted time when we could have been developing other players around Victor, like Devin Vassell. I want this core to evolve together, for Victor to grow with them." ●

"THEY TREAT ME LIKE A MEMBER OF THEIR FAMILY"

"He does everything, which is precisely what I expect of him. He also wants to and has the skills for it. "

SPURS COACH GREGG POPOVICH

"HE'S CREATED A NEW SENSE OF UNITY IN THE CITY"

MAYOR RON NIRENBERG

"It just makes me want to go even higher to beat all these records"

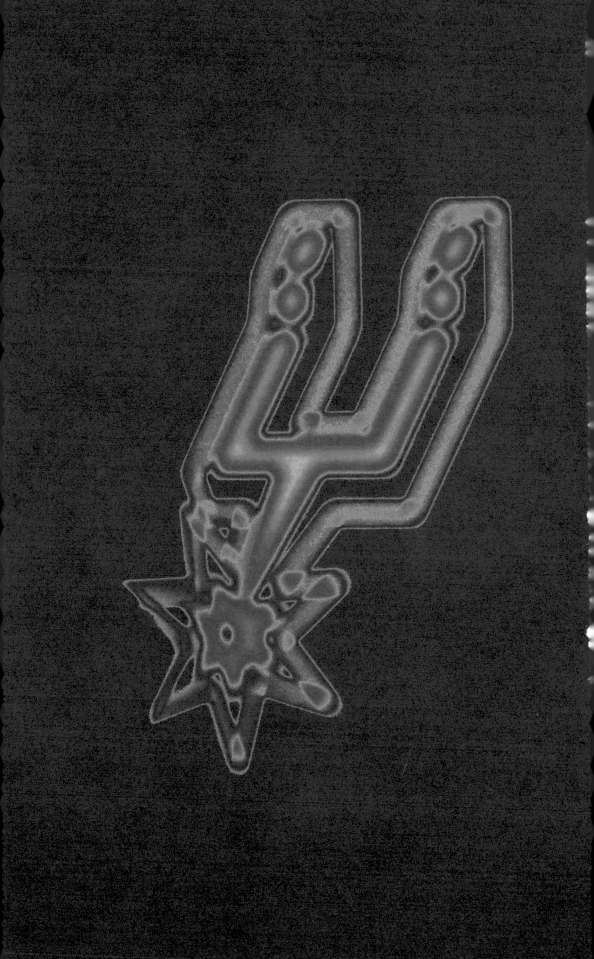

ACKNOWLEDGMENTS

Thank you…

… to Victor Wembanyama and his parents, Élodie de Fautereau and Félix Wembanyama, for accepting our presence alongside them over a number of years, a key condition for being able to report on this unprecedented adventure.

… to Michaël Alard, Guillaume Alquier, Karim Boubekri, Vincent Collet, Frédéric and Pascal Donnadieu, Bryan George, and others from Nanterre and elsewhere, who helped us understand some of the personality of the Spurs "alien."

… to the agency ComSport, Bouna Ndiaye, Jérémy Medjana, and Issa Mboh, for opening many doors for *L'Équipe* despite the media frenzy surrounding their player.

… to Jean-Philippe Bouchard and Laurence Gauthier for believing in this book, and Greg for his remarkable illustrations which took it to another dimension.

… to Julie Dumélié for her assistance and rare photos of the U11 World Cup in Bourbourg.

… to Guillaume Degoulet, Arnaud Lecomte, and Sami Sadik for their willingness to listen and provide assistance, and for allowing me to take some distance from our working lives to devote myself to this project.

… to Pascal Giberné and Maïk Prime for their valuable and inspiring conversations.

… to my lifelong partner, Paula, and my children, Isaac and Gabriel, for putting up with my repeated absences and endless nights of work.

First published in France by Éditions Solar and L'Équipe

First published in Great Britain in 2024 by Cassell, an imprint of
Octopus Publishing Group Ltd
Carmelite House
50 Victoria Embankment
London EC4Y 0DZ

www.octopusbooks.co.uk

An Hachette UK Company
www.hachette.co.uk

All rights of translation, adaptation and reproduction by any means whatsoever reserved for all countries
© Éditions Solar 2023 / © L'Équipe 2023

English translation text copyright © Octopus Publishing Group 2024

Distributed in the US by Hachette Book Group
1290 Avenue of the Americas, 4th and 5th Floors
New York, NY 10104

Distributed in Canada by Canadian Manda Group
664 Annette St., Toronto, Ontario, Canada M6S 2C8

ISBN 978 178840 548 5

A CIP catalogue record for this book is available from the British Library.

Printed and bound in China.

1 3 5 7 9 10 8 6 4 2

All interviews by Yann Ohnona, unless otherwise stated. "Jackpot in Vegas" written by Sami Sadik,
with Arnaud Lecomte and Loïc Pialat. Data compiled by Sami Sadik.

Photo credits

All photos PresseSports, unless otherwise stated. Wembanyama in New York and San Antonio, Sebastien Boué,
except pp.23–24 and 46, Yann Ohnona. French team photos: Sebastien Boué and Franck Faugère.
"Bourbourg: where it all began" chapter, Julie Dumélié. "Jackpot in Vegas" chapter, Xavier de Nauw.
"Alquier, guardian of the treasure" and "When Wemby met Yoda" chapters, Baptiste Paquot.
"A close call with Barça" chapter, ACB. "The secrets of the 'unicorn'" chapter, Alex Martin.
And pp.4–5 and 140–141, Etienne Garnier; pp.132–133, Michaël Alard; pp.142–157 Alexis Réau, *L'Equipe*.

French edition
Art Director, Graphic Designer and Illustrator: Greg @gregartiste
Editor: L'Equipe: Laurence Gauthier, with Jean-Christophe Bassignac
Editorial Director, Solar: Didier Férat
Editor, Solar: Corentin Bréhard

English edition
Publisher: Trevor Davies
Translator: Alison Murray in association with First Edition Translations
Copy Editor: Chris Stone
Designer: Jeremy Tilston
Senior Production Manager: Peter Hunt